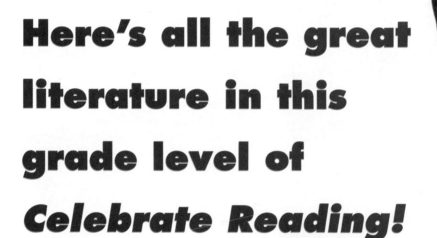

Here's all the great literature in this grade level of *Celebrate Reading!*

Flights of Fancy
Journeys of the Imagination

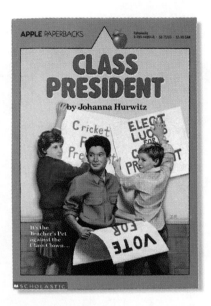

Class President
from the novel by Johanna Hurwitz
✸ Kentucky Bluegrass Award
✸ South Carolina Children's
Book Award

What a Wild Idea
by Louis Sabin

I'm Tipingee, She's Tipingee, We're Tipingee, Too
by Caroline Feller Bauer
✸ Christopher Award Author

The Voice of Africa in American Music
by Jim Haskins
✸ Coretta Scott King Award Author

The Third Gift
by Jan Carew
Illustrations by Leo and Diane Dillon
✸ Caldecott Medal Illustrators

Ashanti to Zulu: African Traditions
from the book by Margaret Musgrove
Illustrations by Leo and Diane Dillon
✸ Boston Globe-Horn Book Award
✸ Caldecott Medal

Mary Poppins
from the novel by P. L. Travers
✸ Nene Award

Catwings
by Ursula K. Le Guin
✸ Children's Choice
✸ Irma Simonton Black Award

Featured Poet
Natalia Belting

Before Your Very Eyes
A World of Nature

Featured Poets
Marilyn Singer
Byrd Baylor
George David Weiss
Bob Thiele

Many People, Many Voices
Stories of America

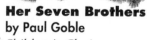

Featured Poets
Duke Redbird
Linh To Sinh My Bui

Within My Reach

The Important Things in Life

Handle with Care

Making a Difference

All About Sam
from the novel by Lois Lowry
✳ Mark Twain Award

Number the Stars
from the novel by Lois Lowry
✳ Newbery Medal
✳ ALA Notable Children's Book
✳ Teachers' Choice
✳ Notable Social Studies Trade Book

Jessi's Secret Language
from the novel by Ann M. Martin
✳ Young Readers' Choice
Award Author

Take a Walk in Their Shoes
from the biography by
Glennette Tilley Turner
✳ Notable Social Studies Trade Book

Meet the Inventor of the Stoplight
by Glennette Tilley Turner

Dorothea Lange: Life Through the Camera
from the biography by
Milton Meltzer
✳ Boston Globe-Horn Book
Award Author

Featured Poets
Ouida Sebestyen
Danny Williams

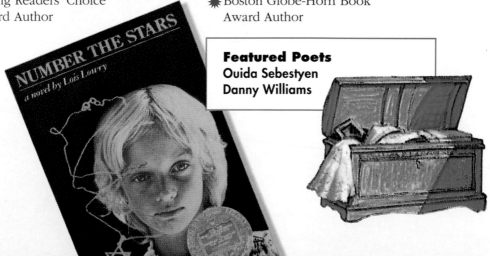

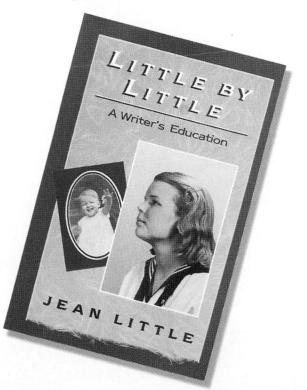

Celebrate Reading!
Trade Book Library

The Great Gerbil Roundup
by Stephen Manes

**Wayside School
Is Falling Down**
by Louis Sachar
☀ Children's Choice
☀ Parents' Choice
☀ Garden State Children's
Book Award

The Year of the Panda
by Miriam Schlein
☀ Outstanding Science Trade
Book for Children

Shiloh
by Phyllis Reynolds Naylor
☀ Newbery Medal

Taking Care of Yoki
by Barbara Campbell

A Lion to Guard Us
by Clyde Robert Bulla
☀ Notable Social Studies Trade Book

The Trading Game
by Alfred Slote
☀ Notable Social Studies Trade Book
☀ Library of Congress
Children's Book

A Taste of Blackberries
by Doris Buchanan Smith
☀ ALA Notable Children's Book
☀ Georgia Children's Book Award

The Pinballs
by Betsy Byars
☀ ALA Notable Children's Book
☀ Children's Book Award
☀ Notable Social Studies
Trade Book
☀ California Young Reader Medal
☀ Library of Congress
Children's Book

Number the Stars
by Lois Lowry
☀ Newbery Medal

The Secret Garden
by Frances Hodgson Burnett
☀ Lewis Carroll Shelf Award

The Noonday Friends
by Mary Stolz
☀ Newbery Medal Honor Book
☀ ALA Notable Children's Book
☀ Library of Congress
Children's Book

Flights of Fancy

Journeys of the Imagination

About the Cover Artist
Johnston Clark used oil paints to create the imaginative cover for
Flights of Fancy. Mr. Clark, a Midwesterner, works at home in a
studio in his basement while his dog Angus snoozes nearby.

ISBN 0-673-81157-3

1997
Scott, Foresman and Company, Glenview, Illinois
All Rights Reserved.
Printed in the United States of America.

Acknowledgments appear on page 136.

12345678910DQ010099989796

Flights of Fancy

JOURNEYS OF THE
IMAGINATION

ScottForesman

A Division of HarperCollinsPublishers

Contents

ON THE WING
GENRE STUDY

STUDENT RESOURCES

Julio, That's Who!

by Johanna Hurwitz

On Monday, Arthur came to school with new glasses. Cricket came to class with a big poster that said,

VOTE FOR CRICKET, THAT'S THE TICKET.

The election was going to be held on Friday. That meant there were only four days more to get ready. In the meantime, they learned about how to make a nomination and how to second it. It was going to be a really serious election.

At lunch, Cricket took out a bag of miniature chocolate bars and gave them out to her classmates. Julio took his and ate it. But it didn't mean he was going to vote for Cricket. He wondered if there was anything Lucas could give out that was better than chocolate. Nothing was better than chocolate!

"If you're going to run against Cricket, we've got to get to work," Julio told Lucas on their way home. Julio wasn't very good at making posters, as Cricket and Zoe were, but he was determined to help his friend.

The next morning, a new poster appeared in Mr. Flores's classroom. It said, DON'T BUG ME. VOTE FOR LUCAS COTT. Julio had made it.

Before lunch, Mr. Flores read an announcement from the principal. "From now on, there is to be no more soccer playing in the schoolyard at lunchtime."

"No more soccer playing?" Julio called out. "Why not?"

Mr. Flores looked at Julio. "If you give me a moment, I'll explain. Mr. Herbertson is concerned about accidents. Last week, Arthur broke his

glasses. Another time, someone might be injured more seriously."

Julio was about to call out again, but he remembered just in time and raised his hand.

"Yes, Julio," said Mr. Flores.

"It's not fair to make us stop playing soccer just because someone *might* get hurt. Someone might fall down walking to school, but we still have to come to school every day."

Julio didn't mean to be funny, but everyone started to laugh. Even Mr. Flores smiled.

"There must be other activities to keep you fellows busy at lunchtime," he said. "Is soccer the only thing you can do?"

Lucas raised his hand. "I don't like jumping rope," he said when the teacher called on him.

All the girls giggled at that.

"You could play jacks," suggested Cricket. Everyone knew it wasn't a serious possibility, though.

"Couldn't we tell Mr. Herbertson that we want to play soccer?" asked Julio.

"You could make an appointment to speak to him, if you'd like," said Mr. Flores. "He might change his decision if you convince him that you are right."

"Lucas and I will talk to him," said Julio. "Right, Lucas?"

"Uh, sure," said Lucas, but he didn't look too sure.

The principal, Mr. Herbertson, spoke in a loud voice and had eyes that seemed to bore right into your head

when he
looked at you. Julio had
been a little bit afraid of Mr. Herbertson
since the very first day of kindergarten. Why had
he offered to go to his office and talk to him?

Mr. Flores sent Julio and Lucas down to the
principal's office with a note, but the principal was
out of the office at a meeting.

"You can talk to him at one o'clock," the
secretary said.

At lunch, Cricket had more chocolate bars. This
time, she had pasted labels on them and printed in tiny
letters, *Cricket is the ticket.* She must be spending her
whole allowance on the campaign, Julio thought.

After a few more days of free chocolate bars,
everyone in the class would be voting for Cricket.

At recess, the girls were jumping rope. You could
fall jumping rope, too, Julio thought.

Back in the classroom, Julio wished he could think
up some good arguments to tell the principal. He looked
over at Lucas. Lucas didn't look very good. Maybe he
was coming down with the flu.

Just before one o'clock, Julio had a great idea.
Cricket was always saying she wanted to be a lawyer.
She always knew what to say in class. Julio figured

she'd know just what to do in the principal's office, too. He raised his hand.

"Mr. Flores, can Cricket go down to Mr. Herbertson's office with Lucas and me? She's running for president, so she should stick up for our class."

"Me?" Cricket said. "I don't care if we can't play soccer."

"Of course," teased Lucas. "You couldn't kick a ball if it was glued to your foot."

"Cricket," said Mr. Flores, "even if you don't want to play soccer, others in the class do. If you are elected, you will be president of the whole class, not just the girls. I think going to the meeting with Mr. Herbertson will be a good opportunity for you to represent the class."

So that was why at one o'clock Julio, Lucas, and Cricket Kaufman went downstairs to the principal's office.

Mr. Herbertson gestured for them to sit in the chairs facing his desk. Cricket looked as pale as Lucas. Maybe she, too, was coming down with the flu.

Julio waited for the future first woman President of the United States to say something, but Cricket didn't say a word. Neither did Lucas. Julio didn't know what to do. They couldn't just sit here and say nothing.

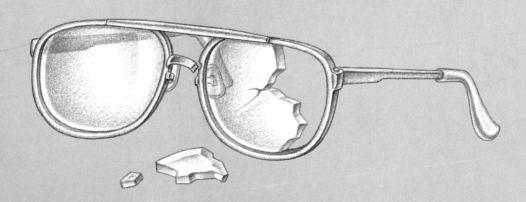

Julio took a deep breath. If Cricket or Lucas wasn't going to talk, he would have to do it. Julio started right in.

"We came to tell you that it isn't fair that no one can play soccer at recess just because Arthur Lewis broke his eyeglasses. Anybody can have an accident. He could have tripped and broken them getting on the school bus." Julio was amazed that so many words had managed to get out of his mouth. No one else said anything, so he went on. "Besides, a girl could fall jumping rope," said Julio. "But you didn't say that they had to stop jumping rope."

"I hadn't thought of that," said Mr. Herbertson.

Cricket looked alarmed. "Can't we jump rope anymore?" she asked.

"I didn't mean that you should make the girls stop jumping rope," Julio went on quickly. He stopped to think of a better example. "Your chair could break while you're sitting on it, Mr. Herbertson," he said.

Mr. Herbertson adjusted himself in his chair. "I certainly hope not," he said, smiling. "What is your name, young man?"

"Julio. Julio Sanchez." He pronounced it in the Spanish way with the *J* having an *H* sound.

"You have a couple of brothers who also attended this school, Julio, don't you?" asked the principal. "Nice fellows. I remember them both."

Julio smiled. He didn't know why he had always been afraid of the principal. He was just like any other person.

"Julio," Mr. Herbertson went on, "you've got a good head on your shoulders, just like your brothers. You made some very good points this afternoon. I think I can arrange things so that there will be more teachers supervising the yard during recess. Then you fellows can play soccer again tomorrow." He turned to Cricket. "You can jump rope if you'd rather do that," he said.

Cricket smiled. She didn't look so pale anymore.

Julio and Lucas and Cricket returned to Mr. Flores's classroom. "It's all arranged," said Cricket as soon as they walked in the door.

The class burst into cheers.

"Good work," said Mr. Flores.

Julio was proud that he had stood up to Mr. Herbertson. However, it wasn't fair that Cricket made it seem as if she had done all the work. She had hardly done a thing. For that matter, Lucas hadn't said anything, either. For a moment, Julio wished he hadn't offered to be Lucas's campaign manager. He wished he was the one running for class president. He knew he could be a good leader.

There was bad news on election day. Chris Willard was absent. Since there were twelve girls and twelve boys in Mr. Flores's class, it meant there were more girls than boys to vote in the election. If all the girls voted for Cricket and all the boys voted for Lucas, there would be a tie. Since one boy was absent, Lucas could be in big trouble. Julio hoped it didn't mean that Lucas had lost the election before they even voted.

Then Mr. Flores told the class that the Parent–Teacher Association was going to be holding a book fair in a few weeks. With more than seventeen dollars from the bake sale, the class could buy a good supply of paperbacks for a special classroom library. Cricket seemed to think it was a great idea, but Julio didn't think it was so hot. After all, there was a school library up one flight of stairs. Why did they need extra books, especially books the students had to pay for out of their *own* money?

Julio thought that the class should vote on the way the money was spent. Before he had a chance to say anything, it was time for lunch.

Lunch was chicken nuggets, whipped potatoes, string beans, and Jell-O squares. Cricket and Zoe didn't even touch their lunches. Julio knew they were talking about the election. Julio clapped Lucas on the back. "You're going to win, pal," he said. "I just know it." He really wasn't so sure, but he felt it was his job to give his candidate confidence. After all, he had convinced Lucas to run for class president in the first place.

Lucas shrugged, trying to act cool. "Maybe yes, maybe no," he said. But Julio could see that he was too excited to eat much lunch, either. Julio polished off his friend's tuna-fish sandwich and his orange. "I need to keep up my strength to vote for you," he told Lucas.

Cricket had more chocolate bars. "Are you going to vote for me?" she asked everyone.

"Maybe yes, maybe no," said Julio, taking his bar.

When they returned from lunch, Mr. Flores called the class to order. It was time for the election to begin. Mr. Flores reminded them about *Robert's Rules of Order,* which was the way school board and other important meetings were conducted.

"You may nominate anyone you choose," he said, "even if your candidate doesn't have a poster up on the wall. Then you can make a speech in favor of your candidate and try to convince your classmates."

Uh-oh, thought Julio. He was ready to nominate Lucas but he didn't know if he would be able to make a speech. He wasn't good with words, as Cricket and Lucas were.

Zoe Mitchell raised her hand. "I nominate Cricket Kaufman," she said. No surprise there. Julio wondered if Zoe had wanted to run herself.

"Does anyone second the nomination?" Mr. Flores asked.

Julio thought the class election sounded like a TV program, not the way people talked in real life.

Sara Jane seconded the nomination, and Mr. Flores wrote Cricket's name on the chalkboard.

"Are there any other nominations?" he asked.

Sara Jane raised her hand again.

"Do you have a question, Sara Jane?" asked Mr. Flores.

"Now I want to nominate Zoe Mitchell."

"You can't nominate someone when you have already seconded the nomination of someone else," Mr. Flores explained. "That's the way parliamentary procedure works."

Cricket looked relieved. She hadn't been expecting any competition from Zoe.

Julio raised his hand. "I nominate Lucas Cott," he said.

"Does anyone second the nomination?"

"Can I second myself?" asked Lucas.

"I'll second the nomination," said Anne Crosby from the back of the classroom.

"Ooooh," giggled one of the girls. "Anne likes Lucas."

"There is no rule that girls can nominate only girls and boys nominate boys," said Mr. Flores. He wrote Lucas's name on the board. "Are there any other nominations?" he asked.

Arthur Lewis raised his hand. "I want to nominate Julio Sanchez," he said.

"Julio?" Sara Jane giggled. "He's just a big goof-off."

"Just a minute," said Mr. Flores sharply. "You are quite out of order, Sara Jane. Does anyone wish to second the nomination?"

Julio couldn't believe that Arthur had nominated him. Even though Arthur had said that Julio should run for president, Julio hadn't thought he would come right out and say it in front of everyone.

Cricket raised her hand. "Julio can't run for president," she said. "He was born in Puerto Rico.

He isn't an
American citizen. You have to be an
American citizen to be elected President. We learned
that last year in social studies."

"Yeah," Lucas called out. "You also have to be thirty-
five years old. You must have been left back a lot of
times, Cricket."

"Hold on," said Mr. Flores. "Are we electing a
President of the United States here, or are we electing
a president of this fifth-grade class?"

Cricket looked embarrassed. It wasn't often she was
wrong about anything.

Julio stood up without even raising his hand.
He didn't care if he was elected president or not, but
there was one thing he had to make clear. "I am so
an American citizen," he said. "All Puerto Ricans are
Americans!"

Julio sat down, and Arthur raised his hand again.
Julio figured he was going to say he had changed his
mind and didn't want to nominate him after all.

"Arthur?" called Mr. Flores.

Arthur stood up. "It doesn't matter where Julio was born," he said. "He'd make a very good class president. He's fair, and he's always doing nice things for people. When I broke my glasses, he was the one who thought of going to Mr. Herbertson so that we could still play soccer at recess. That shows he would make a good president."

"But Julio is not one of the top students like Zoe or Lucas or me," Cricket said.

"He is tops," said Arthur. "He's tops in my book."

Julio felt his ears getting hot with embarrassment. He had never heard Arthur say so much in all the years that he had known him.

"Thank you, Arthur," said Mr. Flores. "That was a very good speech. We still need someone to second the nomination. Do I hear a second?"

Lucas raised his hand.

"I second the nomination of Julio Sanchez," he said.

Mr. Flores turned to write Julio's name on the board. Lucas was still raising his hand.

Mr. Flores turned from the board and called on Lucas again.

"Do you wish to make a campaign speech?" he asked Lucas.

"Yes. I'm going to vote for Julio, and I think everyone else should, too."

"Aren't you even going to vote for yourself?" asked Cricket.

"No," said Lucas. "I want to take my name off the board. Julio is a good leader, like Arthur said. When we went to see Mr. Herbertson, Cricket and I were scared stiff, but Julio just stepped in and did all the talking."

"Are you asking to withdraw your name from nomination, Lucas?" asked Mr. Flores.

"Yes, I am. Everyone who was going to vote for me should vote for Julio."

Julio sat in his seat without moving. He couldn't say a word. He could hardly breathe.

"Are there any other nominations?" asked Mr. Flores.

Zoe raised her hand. "I move that the nominations be closed."

"I second it," said Lucas.

Then Mr. Flores asked the two candidates if they wanted to say anything to the class.

Cricket stood up. "As you all know," she said, "I'm going to run for President of the United States some day. Being class president will be good practice for me. Besides, I know I will do a much, much better job than Julio." Cricket sat down.

Julio stood. "I might vote for Cricket when she runs for President of the United States," he said. "But right now, I hope you will all vote for me. I think our class should make decisions together, like how we should spend the money that we earned at the bake sale. We should spend the money in a way that everyone likes. Not just the teacher." Julio stopped and looked at Mr. Flores. "That's how I feel," he said.

"If I'm president," said Cricket, "I think the money should go to the Humane Society."

"*You* shouldn't tell us what to do with the money, either," said Julio. "It should be a class decision. We all helped to earn it."

"Julio has made a good point," said Mr. Flores. "I guess we can vote on that in the future."

Mr. Flores passed out the ballots. Julio was sure he knew the results even before the votes were counted.

With one boy absent, Cricket would win, twelve to eleven.

Julio was right, and he was wrong. All the boys voted for him, but so did some of the girls. When the votes were counted, there were fourteen for Julio Sanchez and nine for Cricket Kaufman. Julio Sanchez was elected president of his fifth-grade class.

"I think you have made a good choice," said Mr. Flores. "And I know that Cricket will be a very fine vice-president."

Julio beamed. Suddenly he was filled with all sorts of plans for his class.

Mr. Flores took out his guitar. As he had said, they were going to end each week with some singing. Julio thought he had never felt so much like singing in all his life. However, even as he joined the class in the words to the song, he wished it was already time to go home. He could hardly wait to tell his family the news. Wait till he told them who was the fifth-grade class president. Julio, that's who!

At three o'clock, he ran all the way home.

Thinking About It

1. Put yourself in Julio's shoes. You've just been elected president of your class and you weren't even planning to run! Whom will you tell first? What will you tell them you plan to do as president?

2. Will Julio be a good leader or a bad one? Why do you think so? What would you say to defend your opinion?

3. Thirty years have gone by. Julio is running for the office of President of the United States. You are his campaign manager. What will you put on his campaign posters? Why?

Another Book by Johanna Hurwitz
In *Aldo Peanut Butter*, Aldo Sossi has his hands full with the five puppies he gets for his eleventh birthday.

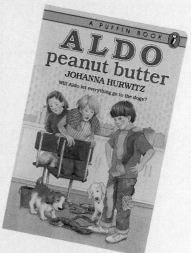

A•25

from *Boys' Life Magazine*

What a Wild Idea

by Louis Sabin

Can you invent a better telephone? Paper clip? Computer gadget? Car engine? If so, fame and fortune could be yours!

But take care. Inventing *useful* things is not easy. Most inventions go no farther than the dusty files of the United States Patent and Trademark Office.

The patent office grants patents, or ownership, for inventions so that other people can't copy them without permission.

The first U.S. patent was granted in 1790. It was for a new way to make potash, an ingredient used to fertilize crops.

More memorable were later inventions, like Thomas Edison's light bulb and Alexander Graham Bell's telephone. Those inventions changed the world.

Other inventions weren't so marvelous. Those go into the "wild idea" category. Take Alfred Clark's Rocking Chair Butter Churn, for example, patented in 1913.

First of all, you have to understand something. Inventions often come from people who hate hard work. They try to find ways to do tough jobs while taking it easy.

No doubt Mr. Clark loved rocking. He probably liked butter too. But in those days, you had to make your own butter, by churning cream. Mr. Clark didn't like that chore, so he combined churning and rocking into one activity.

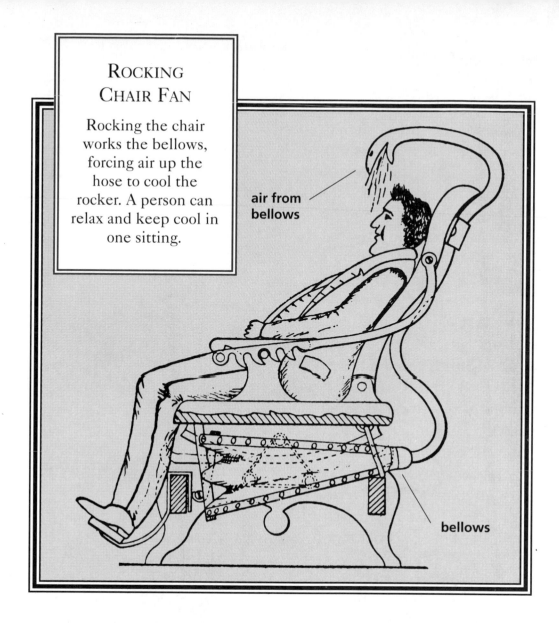

ROCKING CHAIR FAN

Rocking the chair works the bellows, forcing air up the hose to cool the rocker. A person can relax and keep cool in one sitting.

air from bellows

bellows

First, you poured cream into a barrel attached to the chair. Then you sat and rocked. After a while—a *long* while—the cream became butter.

There was nothing wrong with the Rocking Chair Butter Churn, or with its cousins: the Rocking Chair Fan (1869) and the Rocking Chair Washing Machine-Bathtub (1890). Nothing except that doing the rocking was actually harder than doing the work the old-fashioned way.

Lucky for everyone, the electric motor was invented and stopped all rocking chair brainstorms forever.

Round about that time, in 1895, another inventor had a wild idea. James Kelly's invention was a hose-and-ring indoor shower.

It was a simple invention. You just connected the hose to the bathtub faucet and hung the ring around your neck.

The ring had holes in it. Turn on the water and an instant Niagara covered your body. Sounds like a lot of fun, doesn't it? Unfortunately, the public considered the gadget a washout. It disappeared down the drain of time.

Another snoozer was the alarm bed. There were several versions. The first one (patented in 1882) belonged to Samuel S. Applegate.

Mr. Applegate began with a bed and a clock. Connected to the clock was a lever. At wake-up time, the lever moved a wooden arm that pulled a cord. The cord released a wooden frame with 60 corks attached to it. The frame with corks dropped and hit the sleeper's head. The thing was lightweight so as not to cause head injuries.

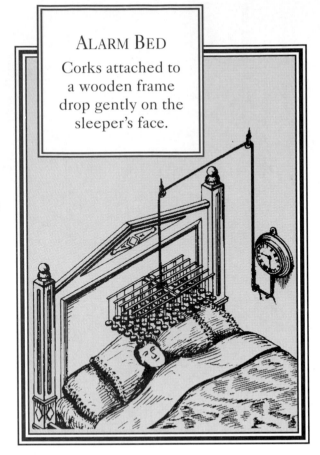

ALARM BED
Corks attached to a wooden frame drop gently on the sleeper's face.

Another wake-up wonder was the Ludwig Ederer Alarm Bed of 1900. It worked with steam. The steam built up pressure in pipes. The pressure made the bed tilt up, sending the sleeper sliding slowly to the floor. He landed just hard enough to wake, without being startled by an alarm. This bold innovation was met with a resounding yawn.

Now you're out of bed and ready for breakfast. Look, it's grapefruit! But wait. Those things are dangerous. They squirt juice in people's eyes—but not if you use Joseph Fallek's 1928 grapefruit shield.

This simple waxed-paper hood fit onto a grapefruit half, held in place by little pins. In position, it looked like a baby carriage without wheels. Brilliant!

That would keep juice out of your eye. But say you want to protect your whole body from splatters. For that, try John Maguire's 1883 Raincoat with Drain.

At first, it looks like an ordinary raincoat. But look closer. The rain collects in a cuff at the bottom. Then it drains away from your pants and shoes through a tube that sticks out one side. It worked—but only in a light rain, when you stood perfectly still.

Okay, you've kept your feet dry. But now you need to get them warm. The obvious choice is William Tell Steiger's 1877 Foot Warmer.

Fit the strap around your neck. Breathe into the little rubber cup. Your warm breath travels down tubes worn

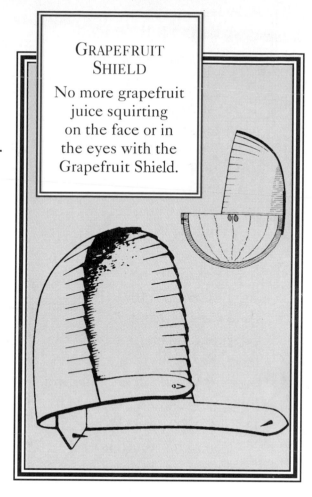

GRAPEFRUIT SHIELD

No more grapefruit juice squirting on the face or in the eyes with the Grapefruit Shield.

under your clothes. The tubes end in your shoes, where your breath heats your feet.

In a crazy way, this one makes sense. But who wants to walk around with a cup at his lip and tubes running down his body? Nobody, that's who. True, you could wear the tubes outside your clothes. But then your breath would cool on the way down.

Not all inventions are for human use, of course. Some are for chickens.

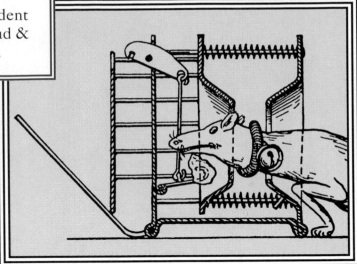

Is your poultry too plump? Your fryer too fat? Then try the hen exerciser, invented by William J. Manly in 1906.

It combines a food box and a tilted, spinning platform. When your hen heads for the food, her weight makes the platform turn. To keep eating, she's got to keep moving. Jogging shoes not included.

You can reward your fit fowl with her own goggles, though. In 1903, Andrew Jackson (no, not *that* Andrew Jackson) invented hen sunglasses. Their purpose? To protect the hen's eyes, of course.

There's an old saying: "Build a better mousetrap and the world will beat a path to your door."

Many have tried. Consider the work of Joseph Barad and Edward E. Markoff, patented in 1908. The trap has a lever in the middle with a bit of cheese on it.

The hungry rodent pokes its head into an opening near the lever. He gets the cheese and trips the lever. This pulls two smaller levers attached to an elastic band with bells on it.

The band snaps around the rodent's neck. It doesn't hurt the animal, just scares him. He rushes back to the nest. The bells scare the other rats. They rush out of the nest. Now that they're out in the open, you can catch them.

How? With your own new, improved Better Mousetrap. The world is waiting. Inventors, get to work!

Thinking About It

1. You've read about several wake-up devices. Which one would you like to have? Why?

2. Think of the inventions mentioned in the article that fit into the "wild idea" category. What are the reasons they never became popular? Now think about the inventions you read about that changed the world. What are the qualities that made them so popular? What can you learn by comparing these lists?

3. Some inventions are supposed to make daily tasks easier. What daily task do you do that an invention could make easier? Describe what the invention would be. Why do you think it would be popular?

Another Book About Inventions

Guess Again: More Weird and Wacky Inventions by Jim Murphy is full of strange and wonderful products of imagination.

I'M
SHE'S
WE'RE

Tipingee, Tipingee, Tipingee, Too

by Caroline Feller Bauer

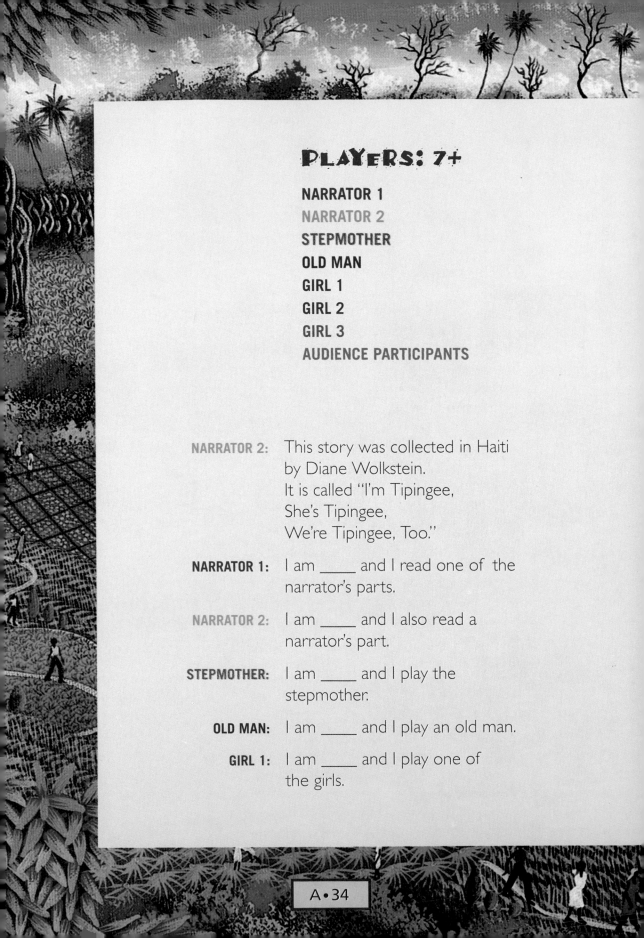

PLAYERS: 7+

NARRATOR 1
NARRATOR 2
STEPMOTHER
OLD MAN
GIRL 1
GIRL 2
GIRL 3
AUDIENCE PARTICIPANTS

NARRATOR 2: This story was collected in Haiti by Diane Wolkstein.
It is called "I'm Tipingee,
She's Tipingee,
We're Tipingee, Too."

NARRATOR 1: I am _____ and I read one of the narrator's parts.

NARRATOR 2: I am _____ and I also read a narrator's part.

STEPMOTHER: I am _____ and I play the stepmother.

OLD MAN: I am _____ and I play an old man.

GIRL 1: I am _____ and I play one of the girls.

GIRL 2:   I am _____ and I play one of the girls.

GIRL 3:   I am _____ and I too play one of the girls.

NARRATOR 1:   There was once a girl named Tipingee. Her stepmother was a selfish woman who didn't like to share her earnings with the girl.

NARRATOR 2:   One day the stepmother needed wood for the fire. She went into the forest to look for firewood. She stood in the middle of the forest and cried out,

STEPMOTHER: My friends, there is so much wood here and at home I have no wood. Who will help me carry the firewood?

NARRATOR 1:   Suddenly, an old man appeared.

OLD MAN: I will help you to carry the firewood. But then what will you give me?

STEPMOTHER: I have very little, but I will find something to give you when we get to my house.

NARRATOR 2:   The old man carried the firewood home for the stepmother.

OLD MAN: I have carried the firewood for you. Now what will you give me?

STEPMOTHER: I will give you a servant girl. I will give you my stepdaughter, Tipingee.

NARRATOR 1: Now Tipingee was in the house, and when she heard her name she ran to the door and listened.

STEPMOTHER: Tomorrow I will send my stepdaughter to the well for water at noon. She will be wearing a red dress. Call her by her name, Tipingee, and she will come to you. Then you can take her.

OLD MAN: Very well. I will do that.

NARRATOR 2: The old man went away.

NARRATOR 1: Tipingee ran to her friends. She ran to the houses of all the girls in her class at school and asked them to wear red dresses the next day.

NARRATOR 2: At noon the next day the old man went to the well. He saw one little girl dressed in red. He saw a second little girl dressed in red. He saw a third little girl dressed in red.

OLD MAN:	Which of you is Tipingee?
GIRL 1:	I'm Tipingee.
GIRL 2:	She's Tipingee.
GIRL 3:	We're Tipingee, too.
OLD MAN:	Which of you is Tipingee?
NARRATOR 1:	The little girls began to clap and jump up and down and chant,
GIRL 1:	I'm Tipingee.
GIRL 2:	She's Tipingee.
GIRL 3:	We're Tipingee, too.
GIRLS 1, 2, 3:	*(clapping and jumping up and down)* I'M TIPINGEE. SHE'S TIPINGEE. WE'RE TIPINGEE, TOO.
NARRATOR 2:	The old man went to the woman.
OLD MAN:	You tricked me. All the girls were dressed in red and each one said she was Tipingee.
STEPMOTHER:	That is impossible. Tomorrow she will wear a black dress. Then you will find her. The one wearing a black dress will be Tipingee. Call her and take her.

NARRATOR 1: But Tipingee heard what her stepmother said and ran and begged all her friends to wear black dresses the next day.

NARRATOR 2: When the old man went to the well the next day, he saw one little girl dressed in black. He saw a second little girl dressed in black. He saw a third girl in black.

OLD MAN: Which of you is Tipingee?

GIRL 1: I'm Tipingee.

GIRL 2: She's Tipingee.

GIRL 3: We're Tipingee, too.

OLD MAN: Which of you is Tipingee?

NARRATOR 1: The girls joined hands and skipped about and sang,

GIRL 1: I'm Tipingee.

GIRL 2: She's Tipingee.

GIRL 3: We're Tipingee, too.

GIRLS 1, 2, 3: (join hands and begin skipping)
I'M TIPINGEE.
SHE'S TIPINGEE.
WE'RE TIPINGEE, TOO.

NARRATOR 2: The man was getting angry. He went to the stepmother.

OLD MAN: You promised to pay me and you are only giving me problems. You tell me Tipingee but everyone here is Tipingee, Tipingee, Tipingee, Tipingee. If this happens a third time, I will come and take you for my servant.

STEPMOTHER: My dear sir, tomorrow she will be in red, completely in red. Call her and take her.

NARRATOR 1: And again Tipingee ran and told her friends to dress in red.

NARRATOR 2: At noon the next day, the old man arrived at the well. He saw one little girl dressed in red. He saw a second little girl dressed in red. He saw a third girl in red.

OLD MAN: Which of you is Tipingee?

GIRL 1: I'm Tipingee.

GIRL 2: She's Tipingee.

GIRL 3: We're Tipingee, too.

OLD MAN: (*shouting*) WHICH OF YOU IS TIPINGEE?

NARRATOR 1: But the girls just clapped and jumped up and down and sang. (*speaking to the audience*) Help us with the chant.

GIRL 1:	I'm Tipingee.
GIRL 2:	She's Tipingee.
GIRL 3:	We're Tipingee, too.
GIRLS 1, 2, 3:	*(begin clapping and jumping up and down)* I'M TIPINGEE. SHE'S TIPINGEE. WE'RE TIPINGEE, TOO.
NARRATOR 2:	The old man knew he would never find Tipingee. He went to the stepmother and took her away. When Tipingee returned home, she was gone. So she lived in her own house with all her father's belongings. She was happy and she sang,
EVERYONE:	I'm Tipingee. She's Tipingee. We're Tipingee, too. I'M TIPINGEE. SHE'S TIPINGEE. WE'RE TIPINGEE, TOO.

THE END

THINKING ABOUT IT

1 You're the director of the play. What stage directions do you have for your actors? What props do you need? What will your sets look like?

2 Why does the author have the girls repeat "I'm Tipingee/She's Tipingee/We're Tipingee, Too" so often throughout the story? What's the effect of the repetition?

3 What advice would you give to help one of these characters solve her problems in a fresh and imaginative way?
> Snow White
> Tipingee
> Cinderella
> Red Riding Hood
> Goldilocks

The Voice of Africa in American Music

by Jim Haskins

You hum, you drum, you tap your feet. You are responding to music, telling yourself and others how you feel. Since history began, music has been a way for groups and nations to share their moods and wishes. Listen to what African American music can tell you. It speaks of hardship and sorrow, of joy and celebration. African music is the root of much of the music that you listen to today.

In Africa:
The World Is Music

Let's try to get a sense of what African music was like long ago. Imagine what you would see and hear if you were to step into a West African village in the 1770s. Women are busy pounding maize or manioc to make a meal, cooking over an open fire, or collecting firewood. Around them are laughing, playing children. Men are setting off to hunt or to clear farmland or herd livestock. Everywhere, there is music and singing. The women sing of the good harvest they hope for; the children keep time by drumming their feet on the hard-packed earth. The men do a special dance for good luck on their hunt. From far off come the sounds of huge drums made from hollowed-out logs and tightly stretched animal skins. The drums announce the approach of a herd of wildebeest or warn of a stampede of elephants. Each series of drumbeats carries a separate message.

Music is not just for special occasions, although there are

A woman dances in a village in Senegal.

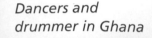

Dancers and drummer in Ghana

special tunes and songs and dances for those. Music is a part of everyday life. Surrounded by gods of the trees and rocks and streams, the villagers spoke to these gods through music. This is a rhythmic music, marked not just by one or two rhythms but by five or more. These rhythms are echoed in dancing, with various parts of the body each moving with one of the rhythms. It is played on other instruments besides drums— on stringed instruments much like the banjo and guitar. It is also "played" with voices, when a group of people sing.

Slavery: Sorrow and Rebellion

When Africans were captured and brought to America on slave ships, they were forced to leave their villages, their families, and their homeland, but they could not be forced to leave their music. Slaves from different villages often spoke different languages. They used music to share their sorrow, to tell each other of their fear and anger. They used their voices to sing and their hands to pound out rhythm on the bottom of a tub or tin kettle.

Once the slaves were sold and taken home with their owners, they used music to express their desire to escape. Their drumbeats were a sort of "Morse code" to send messages. After a series of revolts and escapes, the slave owners outlawed the use of drums, but that did not stop the slaves. Instead they used their feet to tap out messages as they danced.

After being in America for a time, many slaves adopted Christianity as their religion. They often combined parts of their old religions with the new one. Out of this mingling of religions came a music called spirituals. Spirituals were called sorrow songs because they expressed the deep suffering of the slaves.

Mostly, however, the slaves used music to make their burdens lighter and to restore their spirits. In the fields, they sang work songs. Everyone could take part in these songs. A leader would sing one line, and the other workers would

Slaves in America used music and dance to express their desire to escape.

Blues (top) and ragtime (bottom) grew out of plantation spirituals and work songs.

reply with the next. If their hands or feet were free, they would accompany their own singing with clapping or tapping.

Slaves in America made instruments like those they had used in Africa. They used dried animal bones to produce a clacking sound. They made drums from hollowed-out logs or nail kegs, with animal skins stretched tightly across one end. They introduced the banjo to America; the word comes from the African word *banjar.*

Slave bands became a regular part of the entertainment on southern plantations. Generations of white children in the South grew up hearing spirituals sung to them by the black women who cared for them.

The Birth of Blues, Ragtime, and Jazz

When slavery ended, black musicians were able to travel about and perform their music. In the towns along the Mississippi River, they learned from each other and developed a new music that expressed their lives. The blues and ragtime grew out of the old plantation spirituals and work songs.

Blues, like the sorrow songs of the earlier plantation days, were the cries of a people who had little hope. These songs were often sung in lively rhythms—like laughing to keep from crying. Ragtime got its name from the "ragged time" that marks African music.

From blues and ragtime came jazz, which was also born in the southern towns along the Mississippi River. Played by groups of musicians, jazz was marked by distinctive rhythms and by improvisation, or making up the music as one went along. Orchestras in the all-black army regiments that went to Europe during World War I brought jazz with them. It immediately became popular in Europe.

Rock 'n' Roll and Beyond

In the early 1950s a black performer named Bo Diddley was playing music with a strange new sound. On his

1920s Jazz band

Bo Diddley

guitar, he pounded out a beat that many white performers had never heard before. He called it a "basic bottom" beat. Others called it a double-rhythm beat. A disc jockey named Alan Freed decided to call it "rock 'n' roll."

Soon many white musicians were trying this new kind of music. Elvis Presley, the Beatles, and the Rolling Stones all used the sounds of African American blues, jazz, and rock 'n' roll in their music.

The rock music we listen to today has an African beat. In it we can hear the sounds of African drums and banjos. We can hear the voices of workers in the fields of the South. We can hear the improvisations of jazz. We can hear the history of African Americans—if we know how to listen.

Thinking About It

1. "The Voice of Africa in American Music" contains information about the roots of the music that we all listen to. How much of this information was new to you? What in the article surprised you?

2. Explain in what ways this statement is true: Jazz made its way to Europe from Africa by way of the United States.

3. Listen to two pieces of music. Do you hear African roots in them? Try to describe or demonstrate the roots.

Through the Eyes of the Illustrators

by
Leo Dillon
and
Diane Dillon

When you look at a title page in some books, you see the name of an illustrator. We are illustrators. We draw and paint pictures for stories.

Our job as illustrators begins when the publisher sends us the author's story, a manuscript. We read and discuss it and begin to picture illustrations in our minds. This is the exciting first step. We must imagine a world. We must decide what pictures we can create to reflect visually the words of the manuscript.

We read the manuscript many times to make sure we haven't missed any details the author described—the color of someone's eyes, for example. We have to figure out if the story happens all in one day or over several days. Do characters change clothes, or should they keep wearing the same ones? If an author has written *The boy went to his room*, we must understand that story character in order to create his room. Would he have a desk? What would hang on his walls? Is his room messy or neat?

The next step is the scary part: getting our ideas down on paper. Everything is carefully worked out in pencil first. Then we transfer our drawing onto illustration board to do the

finished art in color. We save those pencil drawings, such as the example here from *Ashanti to Zulu*, just in case we have to do it over.

As we decide about the illustrations for each story, we experiment with different techniques because that is how we get our thoughts down on paper. We use watercolor, pastel, acrylic paint, and colored pencils, whatever is best for what we want to do. Sometimes we use all of them on one illustration. That is called mixed media. It takes a lot of practice to get the confidence that the art will come out right.

from Ashanti to Zulu

from
*The Tale of the
Mandarin
Ducks*

One of the first books we illustrated is *Whirlwind Is a Ghost Dancing*. We researched the art of many Native American groups and based our illustrations on their styles. Compare the illustrations on pages A·74 to A·77 in your book. Look for repeated patterns. What differences do you see? Notice how the words of the poem are represented in the illustration. How does the art help you picture what the poem is saying?

Now look at the varied brush lines and soft tones in the illustration above from *The Tale of the Mandarin Ducks*. We spent three weeks of trial and error, experimenting with watercolor and many types of paper to get the effect of a Japanese style of woodblock prints called *ukiyoe* (yü kē′ ō ā′). In these "floating world" prints of two and three centuries ago, artists carved in wood the lines to capture the grace of a brushstroke. We liked the style and wanted to do something that reflected a Japanese feeling.

magine the sights, sounds, and smells of the marketplace when you look below at our illustration for *Two Pair of Shoes*. Can you figure out what we did to call attention to the shoes? For these two short stories from the Middle East, we studied the rich art heritage from that part of the world, especially the Persian miniatures that illustrated ancient books. Seeing these small, fancy figures with brilliant colors and gold backgrounds helps you understand why people in the story would stare at a pair of shabby shoes.

from Two Pair of Shoes

*W*e've done several books with African settings. For *Why Mosquitoes Buzz in People's Ears*, a West African tale shown above, our style was inspired by African *batik* (bə tēk′). In batik, a design is drawn on cloth with wax. Then the cloth is dyed, but the wax prevents the dye from coloring the lines. When the cloth dries and the wax is removed, the lines stand out, usually white against the color.

Notice how our wide white outlines look like a batik design. This book was awarded a Caldecott Medal for "most distinguished American picture book for children" during its year of publication.

If the story takes place in a particular part of Africa, we look at styles of art from that area. We find out whatever we can to create a picture for that place and time. Illustration takes

from *Why Mosquitoes
Buzz in People's Ears*

This is an example of *batik* (bə tēk′).

attention to detail and requires us to observe carefully.

A good example of the importance of detail is our work in *Ashanti to Zulu,* which also received a Caldecott Medal. Look at pages A·78 to A·82 in your book to see what we mean about details. What do you learn about these three groups of people by looking at the illustrations? How do they dress? How do they live their lives? What does their world look like? As you may guess, our research for this book took longer than the art work. We had to get special permission to use the United Nations library in New York to get information about African traditions. Librarians help us a lot.

When we illustrate fantasy or a fairy tale, we don't have to worry about factual details. We can use more of our inventive imagination.

The Third Gift, an African fantasy, gave us freedom to use lush flowing designs and rich colors. We were inspired by art nouveau (ärt nü vō′), an art style that was popular in the 1890s and 1960s. We used the flowing curves, interlaced patterns, and images from nature that are common in art nouveau to give the feeling of the story. How does the illustration on page A·68 in your book help you imagine how the main character was feeling?

For the fantasy *The Porcelain Cat* we could invent the clothing and landscape and use unusual effects with total freedom. For example, look at the expression on the trunk of the tree in the illustration on the next page. For fun we hid cats all through the story. Try to find them in this picture.

Art nouveau uses flowing curves and interlaced patterns.

from *The Porcelain Cat*

Most of our career is based on illustrating literature from many cultures. Each book is different, with its own problems to solve and something new to learn. We are never bored. There are many good careers in art working in offices for companies such as publishers and advertising agencies. We freelance, which means we work in our own studio at home for many different clients. We love what we do—using our imaginations, using a variety of styles and techniques. We feel that we are doing something important, and we hope that it brings joy to people like you.

"Through the Eyes of the Illustrators" by Leo and Diane Dillon. © 1991 by Leo and Diane Dillon.

This is an illustration we did for the cover of Aïda, as told by Leontyne Price.

Thinking About It

1. What might it be like to be a children's book illustrator? Based on what the Dillons say, what would you find enjoyable? Explain your answer.

2. You're going to do a slide show to present the Dillons' work to another class. Which of their illustrations will you include? How did you decide? Prepare what you will say about each of the pictures.

3. Think of one of your favorite books. Suppose you were going to illustrate it. What would you do?

Another Book Illustrated by Leo and Diane Dillon

In *Who's in Rabbit's House?* by Verna Aardema the characters wear masks, and the story is acted out as a play. Look for the lions who play the part of the audience watching in the background.

The Third Gift

by Jan Carew

illustrated by Leo and Diane Dillon

In long-time-past days there was a black prophet named Amakosa who was the leader of the Jubas—a clan of herdsmen and wanderers. When Amakosa felt age nesting inside his tired limbs, and was certain that the soft footsteps he heard following him were those of Mantop, Death's messenger boy, he summoned the elders of the clan to a palaver. It was a time when endless seasons of drought and dust were scattering the Jubas and their herds like silk cotton blossoms in the wind, and the clan was threatened with extinction.

The elders gathered in a circle and drank libations. As the sacred gourd was passed around, dark hands, lean and veined, trembled like leaves.

Amakosa, with his old and cunning eyes gleaming in nests of wrinkled flesh, said calmly, "We must find green pastures, and places where the wind brings rain, and where the vampire sun is no longer king."

"Ai! Ai!," the people said in a chorus, "lead us there and we will follow you."

So the Jubas picked up their belongings and followed Amakosa across the parched savannahs where the wind had bent the thorn trees like old men's backs and where the stunted elephant grass hissed like snakes. Through endless seasons of waxing and waning moons, they left a trail of bones picked clean by vultures and bleached by the sun. One evening, when the gloaming was giving way to starlight and pale lightnings, they came to the foot of a mountain whose peak was lost in the stars. They washed their dirty limbs in cool streams and threw themselves down on the innocent grass, wherever sleep surprised them.

They woke up at day—clean refreshed, and stretching themselves like ocelots, they asked, "What is this mountain called, Amakosa?"

"It has no name, so we will call it Nameless Mountain," Amakosa said.

"And what is this place called, Amakosa?"

"We will call it Arisa, the place of springs."

The Jubas settled in Arisa, and when Mantop, Death's messenger boy, finally knocked on his door, Amakosa called all the Jubas together and said,

"Listen well to what I have to say. My face has beaten against many years, and now Mantop has sent for me. You must choose a leader to succeed me. When I have gone, all the young men must make their way up Nameless Mountain. The one that climbs the highest and brings back a gift of the wonders that he saw, him you must make your leader."

The Jubas were silent when Mantop led

their prophet away. When sunset was casting long shadows, they saw the two—a headless man with a flute stuck in his throat and the old man Amakosa, bent with the weight of his years—walking towards the River of Night. And at day-clean even the wind was heavy with lamentation.

Then all the young men set out up Nameless Mountain—up past the orchids and wild vines on the mossy face of the rocks, up to where the wild mango stripes the slopes with white blossoms, up to where secret springs gurgle into rivers. Up and up they climbed until all they could hear was the wind in the stranger-trees and the echoes of drums on the plains. Towards evening one man came back weary and sleepy as mud, and the others followed dragging their feet. But the one that climbed the highest came running deer-speed down the mountainside holding something in his hand high above his head. He didn't stop until he reached the village square. The Jubas crowded around him and chorused, "Show us the wonderful thing you brought, Brother-Man!"

And the young man said, "Come closer and see." He opened his hand and declared, "This is what I have brought. Eye never saw and hand never touched a gift like this."

And the women cried out with wonder, "Look at the curve of it and the way it catches the light! It is truly a wondrous thing!"

The gift that the young man brought was a stone, and when this stone caught the light, it had all the colors of mountain orchids and rainbows and more.

"But what is the message in this stone?" the people asked.

"This stone brings us the gift of Work," the young man said. "Since we wandered into this green country we have become idle, and idleness is a more terrible threat than drought or hunger."

And looking at the stone all of the Jubas had a vision of ploughshares and axe blades, endless fields of maize and cassava, and harvest times filled with the songless singing of their drums.

Jawa, the man who had brought the gift of Work, ruled for a long time. The Juba nation multiplied, and the memory of hunger and laziness was pushed far away from them.

But the time came when Mantop, Death's messenger boy, knocked on Jawa's door of reeds, and he, too, had to walk the trail to the

River of Night. The lamentation weighed heavy on the hearts of those he left behind.

So, once again at fore-day-morning, the young men set out up Nameless Mountain. And Kabo, the man who climbed the highest this time, came down the mountainside soft-softly. He could not hurry because the gift he brought was a mountain flower. When he stood in the center of the village square holding this marvelous Flower in his hand, it was clear for all to see that he had brought his people the gift of Beauty. They crowded around him to marvel at the curve of the petals and the colors and the way the pistil caught the light and made the pollen glitter like jewels. The singing drums and the song-makers sang Kabo's praises far into the night.

Kabo ruled through many moons, and the Juba country became a place to wonder at. The door of every house had flowers painted on it in bright vermilion colors; the girls wore flowers in their hair; flowers without number were carved out of wood and stone, and every canoe was built with a flower sculpted on its prow.

But, the Jubas grew dissatisfied. They had Work and Beauty and yet they wanted more. Some began to mutter that they were thinking of moving to another country down the river and across the plains. So when Mantop sent for Kabo everyone knew that his successor would

have to bring back a powerful gift from
Nameless Mountain to hold the nation together.

Kabo went on his journey to the River of
Night quietly, and for the third time the young
men set out up Nameless Mountain. Amongst
them was a dreaming, sad-faced son of Tiho
the Hunter who was called Ika, the Quiet One.
Ika always looked as if he was gnawing at the
bones of everlasting griefs.

He took a trail on the far side of Nameless
Mountain where none of the others dared
follow. When night fell and the fireflies
brightened the fields and forests like fallen
stars, everyone returned except Ika.

And the weary ones who had returned said,
"We saw him parting the clouds and climbing
up and up, and none of us had the strength to
follow him."

When Ika did not return by the next
morning, the Jubas sent search parties to look for
him and posted lookouts on the mountainside.
Sun and Moon lengthened many shadows; still
Ika did not return. There was plenty of talk about
him and how he had gone his lonesome way to
die on Nameless Mountain.

But one morning bright with dew and
singing birds, Ika came running down the
mountainside, parting the long grass and
leaping from rock to rock. He was clenching his
fist and holding his hand high above his head.

He reached the river bank and crossed the cassava fields, trampling down the young plants. When he came to the village square he did not stop.

And the people said, "Aye, aye, Ika, you're home, man! We were waiting for you until our hearts were becoming weary with waiting."

But he kept on running, and again they shouted, "You're home, man! Ika, you're home!"

Ika would have run right across the village square and away towards the fields of elephant grass if he had not tripped on a piece of firewood. He fell and lay panting as though his chest was going to burst, still keeping his fist clenched.

"What gift have you brought us, Brother-Man? Talk to us. What did you see above the clouds on Nameless Mountain?"

For a long time Ika could find no words to answer them. But Leza, the Healer, came and anointed him with kuru oil. The men could not wait to see the gift he had brought; so they pried his fist open. But when they opened Ika's hand, it was empty.

When Ika found his tongue again, he said, "I went up to the clouds and over and above them, and I don't know how long it took because past the clouds was a brightness that blinded my eyes. Then there came a time when all I felt was a soft carpet under my feet, and when I breathed in the mountain air, it was like drawing knife blades up my nostrils. When my sight came back I found myself on the mountain top . . ."

"Lord! You must've seen the whole world from there, Ika!" a young man exclaimed.

"Yes, and while I stood up there a soft white thing like rain started to fall . . . and yet it wasn't rain because it fell like leaves when there is no wind. I gathered this downy whiteness in my hand, but the farther down the mountainside I ran, the less of it I was holding, so I went back for more and ran down the mountain again. Four times I did this, and every time I was heading for home bird-speed, this magic thing melted in my hand. All I bring with me now is the memory of it, the feel of the sky and the bite of the wind—and the fire and ice burning my hand."

And the people listening believed, for this quiet young man, when he did speak, could warble like singing-birds-sweet, and when he spoke, his words would grow inside your head like seeds.

Ika became prophet of the Jubas for he had brought the best gift of all, the gift of Fantasy, of Imagination and of Faith. So, with the gifts of Work and Beauty and Imagination, the Jubas became poets and bards and creators, and they live at the foot of Nameless Mountain to this day.

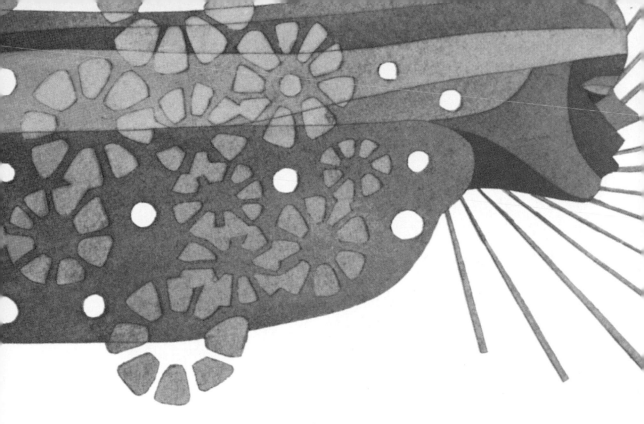

Thinking About It

1. Step into the picture on page A·68 and stand next to Ika. What do you see? How do you feel? Why do you feel that way?

2. *The Third Gift* says the gift of imagination was the best gift of all for the Jubas. What do you see in the illustrations that helps you believe that?

3. If you put the third gift in a package and gave it to someone, how would you wrap it? Why would you wrap it that way?

The Rainbow

from *Whirlwind Is a Ghost Dancing*
by Natalia Belting
illustrated by Leo and Diane Dillon

The sky is a bowl of ice
Turned over above the earth.

The rainbow is a serpent
Rubbing his back against the ice,
Shedding his skin in bits of snow and rain.

Shoshoni
Nevada and Utah

Is a Serpent

Dew Eagle, at night,
Comes out of his lodge west of the sun.
He carries a bowl of water on his back
And spreads cooling dew over the hot earth.

Iroquois
New York

Sun rays shining through the dusty air,
Breaking through the rain clouds,
Are Earth-Maker's eyelashes.

Bella Coola
British Columbia

Lightning is a great giant
Who makes a path through the sky
For the thunderstorm.

His bonnet is feathered clouds.
His blanket is a black cloud.
His moccasins are the swift winds.

He carries the whirlwind like a sack
  slung over his shoulder.
He whips the clouds with his lariat.

Skidi Pawnee
Nebraska

The stars are night birds with bright breasts
Like hummingbirds.

Twinkling stars are birds flying slowly.
Shooting stars are birds darting swiftly.

Taos Pueblo
New Mexico

The sun is a yellow-tipped porcupine
Lolloping through the sky,
Nibbling treetops and grasses and weeds,
Floating on rivers and ponds,
Casting shining barbed quills at the earth.

Crow

Great Plains

Ashanti

by Margaret Musgrove

to Zulu

illustrated by Leo and Diane Dillon

ASHANTI

Ashanti (uh·shahnt·ee) weavers make a
beautiful cloth called *kente.* They weave it
in bright silk threads and give each different
design a name. One, which is mostly yellow,
is called "Gold Dust." Another, called "When
the Queen Comes to Accra," is a favorite of
many Ashanti women. "One Man Cannot
Rule a Country" was designed especially for
Ghana's first president. The Ashanti king
drapes himself in a special *kente* that only
he may wear.

EWE

Ewe (eh´·vay) drummers "talk" with drums.
A long time ago Ewe drums sent news to
people miles and miles away. Today there are
telephones and telegraphs in Africa, but the
drums still "talk." On special occasions the
Ewe drum and dance together. The "talking"
drums tell everyone what the dance is about
and what steps to do. These drums have strings
stretched from top to bottom all around them.
By squeezing the strings against their bodies as
they hit the drums, the drummers can make the
"voices" higher or lower.

OUADAI

A *Ouadai (wah•dy´)* market is held under leaf
canopies. The sun is very hot, so palm leaves
are woven together and stretched over sticks.
Market women sit under these shelters and
sell dates, meat, cloth, and other things. Their
shrill voices call out as their hands and eyes
beckon. Customers must bargain with them
for fair prices. People shake their heads and
walk away, but they come back. Bargaining
is serious business, but it's a lot of fun too.

THINKING ABOUT IT

You are a guest of an Ashanti, Ewe, or Ouadai family. What do you expect to see? What do you expect to do? Why?

The Dillons spend much time researching before they begin their illustrations. Why is accurate research important to their work?

If you were to choose music to go with "The Rainbow Is a Serpent," what would you choose? Why?

ANOTHER CALDECOTT WINNER

Read *Why Mosquitoes Buzz in People's Ears* by Verna Aardema to see another example of how the Dillons fit an art style to a story.

Why Mosquitoes Buzz in People's Ears
Verna Aardema | pictures by
Leo and Diane Dillon

Laughing Gas

from Mary Poppins

by P. L. Travers

"Are you quite sure he will be at home?" said Jane, as they got off the Bus, she and Michael and Mary Poppins.

"Would my uncle ask me to bring you to tea if he intended to go out, I'd like to know?" said Mary Poppins, who was evidently very offended by the question. She was wearing her blue coat with the silver buttons and the blue hat to match, and on the days when she wore these it was the easiest thing in the world to offend her.

All three of them were on the way to pay a visit to Mary Poppins's uncle, Mr. Wigg, and Jane and Michael had looked forward to the trip for so long that they were more than half afraid that Mr. Wigg might not be in, after all.

"Why is he called Mr. Wigg—does he wear one?" asked Michael, hurrying along beside Mary Poppins.

"He is called Mr. Wigg because Mr. Wigg is his name. And he doesn't wear one. He is bald," said Mary Poppins. "And if I have any more questions we will just go Back Home." And she sniffed her usual sniff of displeasure.

Jane and Michael looked at each other and frowned. And the frown meant: "Don't let's ask her anything else or we'll never get there."

Mary Poppins put her hat straight at the Tobacconist's Shop at the corner. It had one of those curious windows where there seem to be three of you instead of one, so that if you look long enough at them you begin to feel you are not yourself but a whole crowd of somebody else. Mary Poppins sighed with pleasure, however, when she saw three of herself, each wearing a blue coat with silver buttons and a blue hat to match. She thought it was such a lovely sight that she wished there had been a dozen of her or even thirty. The more Mary Poppins the better.

"Come along," she said sternly, as though they had kept *her* waiting. Then they turned the corner and pulled the bell of Number Three, Robertson Road. Jane and Michael could hear it faintly echoing from a long way away and they knew that in one minute, or two at the most, they would be having tea with Mary Poppins's uncle, Mr. Wigg, for the first time ever.

"If he's in, of course," Jane said to Michael in a whisper.

At that moment the door flew open and a thin, watery-looking lady appeared.

"Is he in?" said Michael quickly.

"I'll thank you," said Mary Poppins, giving him a terrible glance, "to let *me* do the talking."

"How do you do, Mrs. Wigg," said Jane politely.

"Mrs. Wigg!" said the thin lady, in a voice even thinner than herself. "How dare you call me Mrs. Wigg? No, thank you! I'm plain Miss Persimmon *and* proud of it. Mrs. Wigg indeed!" She seemed to be quite upset, and they thought Mr. Wigg must be a very odd person if Miss Persimmon was so glad not to be Mrs. Wigg.

"Straight up and first door on the landing," said Miss Persimmon, and she went hurrying away down the passage saying: "Mrs. Wigg indeed!" to herself in a high, thin, outraged voice.

Jane and Michael followed Mary Poppins upstairs. Mary Poppins knocked at the door.

"Come in! Come in! And welcome!" called a loud, cheery voice from inside. Jane's heart was pitter-pattering with excitement.

"He *is* in!" she signalled to Michael with a look.

Mary Poppins opened the door and pushed them in front of her. A large cheerful room lay before them. At one end of it a fire was burning brightly and in the center stood an enormous table laid for tea—four cups and saucers, piles of bread and butter, crumpets, coconut cakes and a large plum cake with pink icing.

"Well, this is indeed a Pleasure," a huge voice greeted them, and Jane and Michael looked round for its owner. He was nowhere to be seen. The room appeared to be quite empty. Then they heard Mary Poppins saying crossly:

"Oh, Uncle Albert—not *again?* It's not your birthday, is it?"

And as she spoke she looked up at the ceiling. Jane and Michael looked up too and to their surprise saw a round, fat, bald man who was hanging in the air without holding on to anything. Indeed, he appeared to be *sitting* on the air, for his legs were crossed and he had just put down the newspaper which he had been reading when they came in.

"My dear," said Mr. Wigg, smiling down at the children, and looking apologetically at Mary Poppins, "I'm very sorry, but I'm afraid it *is* my birthday."

"Tch, tch, tch!" said Mary Poppins.

"I only remembered last night and there was no time then to send you a postcard asking you to come another day. Very distressing, isn't it?" he said, looking down at Jane and Michael.

"I can see you're rather surprised," said Mr. Wigg. And, indeed, their mouths were so wide open with astonishment that Mr. Wigg, if he had been a little smaller, might almost have fallen into one of them.

"I'd better explain, I think," Mr. Wigg went on

calmly. "You see, it's this way. I'm a cheerful sort of man and very disposed to laughter. You wouldn't believe, either of you, the number of things that strike me as being funny. I can laugh at pretty nearly everything, I can."

And with that Mr. Wigg began to bob up and down, shaking with laughter at the thought of his own cheerfulness.

"Uncle Albert!" said Mary Poppins, and Mr. Wigg stopped laughing with a jerk.

"Oh, beg pardon, my dear. Where was I? Oh, yes. Well, the funny thing about me is—all right, Mary, I won't laugh if I can help it!—that whenever my birthday falls on a Friday, well, it's all up with me. Absolutely U.P.," said Mr. Wigg.

"But why——?" began Jane.

"But how——?" began Michael.

"Well, you see, if I laugh on that particular day I become so filled with Laughing Gas that I simply can't keep on the ground. Even if I smile it happens. The first funny thought, and I'm up like a balloon. And until I can think of something serious I can't get down again." Mr. Wigg began to chuckle at that, but he caught sight of Mary Poppins's face and stopped the chuckle, and continued:

"It's awkward, of course, but not unpleasant. Never happens to either of you, I suppose?"

Jane and Michael shook their heads.

"No, I thought not. It seems to be my own special habit. Once, after I'd been to the Circus the night before, I laughed so much that—would you believe it?—I was up here for a whole twelve hours, and couldn't get down till the last stroke of midnight. Then, of course, I came down with a flop because it was Saturday and not my birthday anymore. It's rather odd, isn't it? Not to say funny?

"And now here it is Friday again and my birthday, and you two and Mary P. to visit me. Oh, Lordy, Lordy, don't make me laugh, I beg of you——" But although Jane and Michael had done nothing very amusing, except to stare at him in astonishment, Mr. Wigg began to laugh again loudly, and as he laughed he went bouncing and bobbing about in the air, with the newspaper rattling in his hand and his spectacles half on and half off his nose.

He looked so comic, floundering in the air like a great human bubble, clutching at the ceiling sometimes and sometimes at the gas-bracket as he passed it, that Jane and Michael, though they were trying hard to be polite, just couldn't help doing what they did. They laughed. *And* they laughed. They shut their mouths tight to prevent the laughter escaping, but that didn't do any good. And presently they were rolling over and over on the floor, squealing and shrieking with laughter.

"Really!" said Mary Poppins. "Really, *such* behavior!"

"I can't help it, I can't help it!" shrieked Michael as he rolled into the fender. "It's so terribly funny. Oh, Jane, *isn't* it funny?"

Jane did not reply, for a curious thing was happening to her. As she laughed she felt herself growing lighter and lighter, just as though she were being pumped full of air. It was a curious and delicious feeling and it made her want to laugh all the more. And then suddenly, with a bouncing bound, she felt herself jumping through the air. Michael, to his astonishment, saw her go soaring up through the room. With a little bump her head touched the ceiling and then she went bouncing along it till she reached Mr. Wigg.

"Well!" said Mr. Wigg, looking very surprised indeed. "Don't tell me it's *your* birthday, too?" Jane shook her head.

"It's not? Then this Laughing Gas must be catching! Hi—whoa there, look out for the mantelpiece!" This was to Michael, who had suddenly risen from the floor and was swooping through the air, roaring with laughter, and just grazing the china ornaments on the mantelpiece as he passed. He landed with a bounce right on Mr. Wigg's knee.

"How do you do," said Mr. Wigg, heartily shaking Michael by the hand. "I call this really friendly of you—bless my soul, I do! To come up to me since I couldn't come down to you—eh?" And then he and Michael looked at each other and flung back their heads and simply howled with laughter.

"I say," said Mr. Wigg to Jane, as he wiped his eyes. "You'll be thinking I have the worst manners in the world. You're standing and you ought to be sitting—a nice young lady like you. I'm afraid I can't offer you a chair up here, but I think you'll find the air quite comfortable to sit on. I do."

Jane tried it and found she could sit down quite comfortably on the air. She took off her hat and laid it down beside her and it hung there in space without any support at all.

"That's right," said Mr. Wigg. Then he turned and looked down at Mary Poppins.

"Well, Mary, we're fixed. And now I can enquire about *you,* my dear. I must say, I am very glad to welcome you and my two young friends here today—why, Mary, you're frowning. I'm afraid you don't approve of—er—all this."

He waved his hand at Jane and Michael, and said hurriedly:

"I apologize, Mary, my dear. But you know how it is with me. Still, I must say I never thought my two young friends here would catch it, really I didn't, Mary! I suppose I should have asked them for another day or tried to think of something sad or something——"

"Well, I must say," said Mary Poppins primly, "that I have never in my life seen such a sight. And at your age, Uncle——"

"Mary Poppins, Mary Poppins, do come up!" interrupted Michael. "Think of something funny and you'll find it's quite easy."

"Ah, now do, Mary!" said Mr. Wigg persuasively.

"We're lonely up here without you!" said Jane, and held out her arms towards Mary Poppins. *"Do* think of something funny!"

"Ah, *she* doesn't need to," said Mr. Wigg sighing. "She can come up if she wants to, even without laughing—and she knows it." And he looked mysteriously and secretly at Mary Poppins as she stood down there on the hearth-rug.

"Well," said Mary Poppins, "it's all very silly and undignified, but, since you're all up there and don't seem able to get down, I suppose I'd better come up, too."

With that, to the surprise of Jane and Michael, she put her hands down at her sides and without a laugh, without even the faintest glimmer of a smile, she shot up through the air and sat down beside Jane.

"How many times, I should like to know," she said snappily, "have I told you to take off your coat when you come into a hot room?" And she unbuttoned Jane's coat and laid it neatly on the air beside the hat.

"That's right, Mary, that's right," said Mr. Wigg contentedly, as he leant down and put his spectacles on the mantelpiece. "Now we're all comfortable——"

"There's comfort *and* comfort," sniffed Mary Poppins.

"And we can have tea," Mr. Wigg went on, apparently not noticing her remark. And then a startled look came over his face.

"My goodness!" he said. "How dreadful! I've just realized—that table's down there and we're up here. What *are* we going to do? We're here and it's there. It's an awful tragedy—awful! But oh, it's terribly comic!" And he hid his face in his handkerchief and laughed loudly into it. Jane and Michael, though they did not want to miss the crumpets and the cakes, couldn't help laughing too, because Mr. Wigg's mirth was so infectious.

Mr. Wigg dried his eyes.

"There's only one thing for it," he said. "We must think of something serious. Something sad, very sad. And then we shall be able to get down. Now—one, two, three! Something *very* sad, mind you!"

They thought and thought, with their chins on their hands.

Michael thought of school, and that one day he would have to go there. But even that seemed funny today and he had to laugh.

Jane thought: "I shall be grown up in another fourteen years!" But that didn't sound sad at all but quite nice and rather funny. She could not help smiling at the thought of herself grown up, with long skirts and a hand-bag.

"There was my poor old Aunt Emily," thought Mr. Wigg out loud. "She was run over by an omnibus. Sad. Very sad. Unbearably sad. Poor Aunt Emily. But they saved her umbrella. That was funny, wasn't it?" And before he knew where he was, he was heaving and trembling and bursting with laughter at the thought of Aunt Emily's umbrella.

"It's no good," he said, blowing his nose. "I give it up. And my young friends here seem to be no better at sadness than I am. Mary, can't *you* do something? We want our tea."

To this day Jane and Michael cannot be sure of what happened then. All they know for certain is that, as soon as Mr. Wigg had appealed to Mary

**There they were, all together,
up in the air**

Poppins, the table below began to wriggle on
its legs. Presently it was swaying dangerously, and
then with a rattle of china and with cakes lurching
off their plates onto the cloth, the table came
soaring through the room, gave one graceful turn,
and landed beside them so that Mr. Wigg was at
its head.

"Good girl!" said Mr. Wigg, smiling proudly
upon her. "I knew you'd fix something. Now, will
you take the foot of the table and pour out, Mary?
And the guests on either side of me. That's the
idea," he said, as Michael ran bobbing through the
air and sat down on Mr. Wigg's right. Jane was at
his left hand. There they were, all together, up in
the air and the table between them. Not a single

piece of bread-and-butter or a lump of sugar had been left behind.

Mr. Wigg smiled contentedly.

"It is usual, I think, to begin with bread-and-butter," he said to Jane and Michael, "but as it's my birthday we will begin the wrong way—which I always think is the *right* way—with the Cake!"

And he cut a large slice for everybody.

"More tea?" he said to Jane. But before she had time to reply there was a quick, sharp knock at the door.

"Come in!" called Mr. Wigg.

The door opened, and there stood Miss Persimmon with a jug of hot water on a tray.

"I thought, Mr. Wigg," she began, looking searchingly round the room, "you'd be wanting some more hot—— Well, I never! I simply *never!*" she said, as she caught sight of them all seated on the air round the table. "Such goings on I never did see. In all my born days I never saw such. I'm sure, Mr. Wigg, I always knew *you* were a bit odd. But I've closed my eyes to it—being as how you paid your rent regular. But such behavior as this—having tea in the air with your guests—Mr. Wigg, sir, I'm astonished at you! It's that undignified, and for a gentleman of your age—I never did——"

"But perhaps you will, Miss Persimmon!" said Michael.

"Will what?" said Miss Persimmon haughtily.

"Catch the Laughing Gas, as we did," said Michael.

Miss Persimmon flung back her head scornfully.

"I hope, young man," she retorted, "I have more respect for myself than to go bouncing about in the air like a rubber ball on the end of a bat. I'll stay on my own feet, thank you, or my name's not Amy Persimmon, and—oh dear, oh *dear*, my goodness, oh *DEAR*—what *is* the matter? I can't walk, I'm going, I—oh, help, *HELP!*"

For Miss Persimmon, quite against her will, was off the ground and was stumbling through the air, rolling from side to side like a very thin barrel, balancing the tray in her hand. She was almost weeping with distress as she arrived at the table and put down her jug of hot water.

"Thank you," said Mary Poppins in a calm, very polite voice.

Then Miss Persimmon turned and went wafting down again, murmuring as she went: "So undignified—and me a well-behaved, steady-going woman. I must see a doctor——"

When she touched the floor she ran hurriedly out of the room, wringing her hands, and not giving a single glance backwards.

"So undignified!" they heard her moaning as she shut the door behind her.

"Her name can't be Amy Persimmon, because she *didn't* stay on her own feet!" whispered Jane to Michael.

But Mr. Wigg was looking at Mary Poppins —
a curious look, half-amused, half-accusing.

"Mary, Mary, you shouldn't—bless my soul,
you shouldn't, Mary. The poor old body will never
get over it. But, oh, my Goodness, didn't she look
funny waddling through the air—my Gracious
Goodness, but didn't she?"

And he and Jane and Michael were off again,
rolling about the air, clutching their sides and
gasping with laughter at the thought of how funny
Miss Persimmon had looked.

"Oh dear!" said Michael. "Don't make me
laugh any more. I can't stand it! I shall break!"

"Oh, oh, oh!" cried Jane, as she gasped for
breath, with her hand over her heart. "Oh, my
Gracious, Glorious, Galumphing Goodness!"
roared Mr. Wigg, dabbing his eyes with the tail of
his coat because he couldn't find his handkerchief.

"IT IS TIME TO GO HOME." Mary
Poppins's voice sounded above the roars of laughter
like a trumpet.

And suddenly, with a rush, Jane and Michael
and Mr. Wigg came down. They landed on the
floor with a huge bump, all together. The thought
that they would have to go home was the first sad
thought of the afternoon, and the moment it was
in their minds the Laughing Gas went out of them.

Jane and Michael sighed as they watched Mary
Poppins come slowly down the air, carrying Jane's
coat and hat.

Mr. Wigg sighed, too. A great, long, heavy sigh.

"Well, isn't that a pity?" he said soberly. "It's
very sad that you've got to go home. I never
enjoyed an afternoon so much—did you?"

"Never," said Michael sadly, feeling how dull it was to be down on the earth again with no Laughing Gas inside him.

"Never, never," said Jane, as she stood on tiptoe and kissed Mr. Wigg's withered-apple cheeks. "Never, never, never, never . . . !"

They sat on either side of Mary Poppins going home in the Bus. They were both very quiet, thinking over the lovely afternoon. Presently Michael said sleepily to Mary Poppins:

"How often does your uncle get like that?"

"Like what?" said Mary Poppins sharply, as though Michael had deliberately said something to offend her.

"Well—all bouncy and boundy and laughing and going up in the air."

"Up in the air?" Mary Poppins's voice was high and angry. "What do you mean, pray, up in the air?"

Jane tried to explain.

"Michael means—is your uncle often full of Laughing Gas, and does he often go rolling and bobbing about on the ceiling when——"

"Rolling and bobbing! What an idea! Rolling and bobbing on the ceiling! You'll be telling me next he's a balloon!" Mary Poppins gave an offended sniff.

"But he did!" said Michael. "We saw him."

"What, roll and bob? How dare you! I'll have you know that my uncle is a sober, honest, hard-working man, and you'll be kind enough to speak of him respectfully. And don't bite your Bus ticket! Roll and bob, indeed—the idea!"

Michael and Jane looked across Mary Poppins at each other. They said nothing, for they had learnt that it was better not to argue with Mary Poppins, no matter how odd anything seemed.

But the look that passed between them said: "Is it true or isn't it? About Mr. Wigg. Is Mary Poppins right or are we?"

But there was nobody to give them the right answer.

The Bus roared on, wildly lurching and bounding.

Mary Poppins sat between them, offended and silent, and presently, because they were very tired, they crept closer to her and leant up against her sides and fell asleep, still wondering . . .

Crept closer to her and fell asleep

A Word from the Author

MARY POPPINS OPENS THE DOOR P. L. Travers 0-440-40432-0

Mary Poppins Comes Back ✦ P. L. TRAVERS

Mary Poppins P. L. TRAVERS

How Did ★ Mary Poppins Find Me?

from *Cricket Magazine*

by P. L. Travers

Where do ideas come from? Have you any idea where you get an idea? So many people—many of them children—have asked me where I got the idea for Mary Poppins. They want to know whether she is taken from somebody in real life, or whether she is just invented. But how could she be taken from somebody in real life? Did *you* ever know anybody who slid *up* the banisters? On the other hand, who could have "just invented" somebody who slides up banisters and flies from place to place with no other means of propulsion than a parrot-headed umbrella?

These are tricky questions, and I never knew how to answer them till Hendrik Willem van Loon, who wrote and drew so many things for children, came hurrying to my rescue. "No one thought her up," he told me. "She's an idea that came looking for *you!*" And as he was speaking, the idea of three dancing elephants apparently came looking for him, for he drew them for me on the back of an envelope.

But why me? I wanted to know. Why didn't she happen to somebody else? And then I remembered that a boy of sixteen had once asked me to promise him never to become clever. Well, it was a strange request but one I could readily agree to— though of course I wanted to know what he meant. "I've just been reading *Mary Poppins* again," he told me, "and it could only have been written by a special sort of lunatic!"

Well, in a way I understood. To think things up you have to be clever. But to sit still and let them happen to you clearly needs something else. Maybe a kind of listening. Perhaps Lewis Carroll sat still and listened and the idea of *Alice in Wonderland* came by and tapped him on the shoulder. Perhaps the world is full of ideas, all of them looking for the right person. If so, all you

have to do—in addition to being a lunatic—is simply to sit quite still and listen and one of them may happen to you.

Mary Poppins books by P. L. Travers, illustrated by Mary Shepard:

★ *Mary Poppins*
★ *Mary Poppins Comes Back*
★ *Mary Poppins Opens the Door*
★ *Mary Poppins in the Park*
★ *Mary Poppins from A to Z*
★ *Mary Poppins in Cherry Tree Lane*
★ *Mary Poppins and the House Next Door*

Thinking About It

1. If Mary Poppins came to your home, whom would she take care of and what would she do?

2. There is no doubt about it, Mary Poppins is one of the most famous baby-sitters of all time. Interview her. Find out her rules for behavior and her special talents.

3. What do you think will happen next time Mary Poppins takes the children on an outing? Explain why.

Another Book of Fantasy

The Borrowers by Mary Norton is another example of a fantasy. In this story, tiny people borrow what they need from the unsuspecting humans in their house.

CATWINGS

by Ursula K. Le Guin

illustrated by S. D. Schindler

Mrs. Jane Tabby could not explain why all four of her children had wings.

"I suppose their father was a fly-by-night," a neighbor said, and laughed unpleasantly, sneaking round the dumpster.

"Maybe they have wings because I dreamed, before they were born, that I could fly away from this neighborhood," said Mrs. Jane Tabby. "Thelma, your face is dirty; wash it. Roger, stop hitting James. Harriet, when you purr, you should close your eyes part way and knead me with your front paws; yes, that's the way. How is the milk this morning, children?"

"It's very good, Mother, thank you," they answered happily. They were beautiful children, well brought up. But Mrs. Tabby worried about them secretly. It really was a terrible neighborhood, and getting worse. Car wheels and truck wheels rolling past all day—rubbish and litter—hungry dogs— endless shoes and boots walking, running, stamping, kicking—nowhere safe and quiet, and less and less to eat. Most of the sparrows had moved away. The rats were fierce and dangerous; the mice were shy and scrawny.

So the children's wings were the least of Mrs. Tabby's worries. She washed those silky wings every day, along with chins and paws and tails, and

wondered about them now and then, but she worked too hard finding food and bringing up the family to think much about things she didn't understand.

But when the huge dog chased little Harriet and cornered her behind the garbage can, lunging at her with open, white-toothed jaws, and Harriet with one desperate mew flew straight up into the air and over the dog's staring head and lighted on a rooftop—then Mrs. Tabby understood.

The dog went off growling, its tail between its legs.

"Come down now, Harriet," her mother called. "Children, come here please, all of you."

They all came back to the dumpster. Harriet was still trembling. The others all purred with her till she was calm, and then Mrs. Jane Tabby said: "Children, I dreamed a dream before you were born, and I see now what it meant. This is not a good place to grow up in, and you have wings to fly from it. I want you to do that. I know you've been practicing. I saw James flying across the alley last night—and yes, I saw you doing

nose dives, too, Roger. I think you are ready. I want you to have a good dinner and fly away—far away."

"But Mother—" said Thelma, and burst into tears.

"I have no wish to leave," said Mrs. Tabby quietly. "My work is here. Mr. Tom Jones proposed to me last night, and I intend to accept him. I don't want you children underfoot!"

All the children wept, but they knew that that is the way it must be, in cat families. They were proud, too, that their mother trusted them to look after themselves. So all together they had a good dinner from the garbage can that the dog had knocked over. Then Thelma, Roger, James, and Harriet purred goodbye to their dear mother, and one after another they spread their wings and flew up, over the alley, over the roofs, away.

Mrs. Jane Tabby watched them. Her heart was full of fear and pride.

"They are remarkable children, Jane," said Mr. Tom Jones in his soft, deep voice.

"Ours will be remarkable too, Tom," said Mrs. Tabby.

As Thelma, Roger, James, and Harriet flew on, all they could see beneath them, mile after mile, was the city's roofs, the city's streets.

A pigeon came swooping up to join them. It flew along with them, peering at them uneasily from its little, round, red eye. "What kind of birds are you, anyways?" it finally asked.

"Passenger pigeons," James said promptly.

Harriet mewed with laughter.

The pigeon jumped in mid-air, stared at her, and then turned and swooped away from them in a great, quick curve.

"I wish I could fly like that," said Roger.

"Pigeons are really dumb," James muttered.

"But my wings ache already," Roger said, and Thelma said, "So do mine. Let's land somewhere and rest."

Little Harriet was already heading down towards a church steeple.

They clung to the carvings on the church roof, and got a drink of water from the roof gutters.

"Sitting in the catbird seat!" sang Harriet, perched on a pinnacle.

"It looks different over there," said Thelma, pointing her nose to the west. "It looks softer."

They all gazed earnestly westward, but cats don't
see the distance clearly.

"Well, if it's different, let's try it," said James, and
they set off again. They could not fly with untiring
ease, like the pigeons. Mrs. Tabby had always seen to
it that they ate well, and so they were quite plump, and
had to beat their wings hard to keep their weight aloft.
They learned how to glide, not beating their wings,
letting the wind bear them up; but Harriet found
gliding difficult, and wobbled badly.

After another hour or so they landed on the roof
of a huge factory, even though the air there smelled
terrible, and there they slept for a while in a weary,
furry heap. Then, towards nightfall, very hungry—for

nothing gives an appetite like flying—they woke and flew on.

The sun set. The city lights came on, long strings and chains of lights below them, stretching out towards darkness. Towards darkness they flew, and at last, when around them and under them everything was dark except for one light twinkling over the hill, they descended slowly from the air and landed on the ground.

A soft ground—a strange ground! The only ground they knew was pavement, asphalt, cement. This was all new to them, dirt, earth, dead leaves, grass, twigs, mushrooms, worms. It all smelled extremely interesting. A little creek ran nearby. They heard the song of it and went to drink, for they were very thirsty. After drinking, Roger stayed crouching on the bank, his nose almost in the water, his eyes gazing.

"What's that in the water?" he whispered.

The others came and gazed. They could just make out something moving in the water, in the starlight— a silvery flicker, a gleam. Roger's paw shot out . . . .

"I think it's dinner," he said.

After dinner, they curled up together again under a bush and fell asleep. But first Thelma, then Roger, then James, and then small Harriet, would lift their head, open an eye, listen a moment, on guard. They knew they had come to a much better place than the alley, but they also knew that every place is dangerous, whether you are a fish, or a cat, or even a cat with wings.

"It's absolutely unfair," the thrush cried.

"Unjust!" the finch agreed.

"Intolerable!" yelled the bluejay.

"I don't see why," a mouse said. "You've always had wings. Now they do. What's unfair about that?"

The fish in the creek said nothing. Fish never do. Few people know what fish think about injustice, or anything else.

"I was bringing a twig to the nest just this morning, and a *cat* flew down, a cat *flew* down, from the top of the Home Oak, and *grinned* at me in mid-air!" the thrush said, and all the other songbirds cried, "Shocking! Unheard of! Not allowed!"

"You could try tunnels," said the mouse, and trotted off.

The birds had to learn to get along with the Flying Tabbies. Most of the birds, in fact, were more frightened and outraged than really endangered, since they were far better flyers than Roger, Thelma, Harriet, and James. The birds never got their wings tangled up in pine branches and never absent-mindedly bumped into tree trunks, and when pursued they could escape by speeding up or taking evasive action. But they were alarmed, and with good cause, about their fledglings. Many birds had eggs in the nest now; when

the babies hatched, how could they be kept safe from
a cat who could fly up and perch on the slenderest
branch, among the thickest leaves?

It took a while for the Owl to understand this.
Owl is not a quick thinker. She is a long thinker. It
was late in spring, one evening, when she was gazing
fondly at her two new owlets, that she saw James
flitting by, chasing bats. And she slowly thought,
"This will not do . . . ."

And softly Owl spread her great, gray wings, and
silently flew after James, her talons opening.

The Flying Tabbies had made their nest in a hole
halfway up a big elm, above fox and coyote level and
too small for raccoons to get into.
Thelma and Harriet were washing each
other's necks and talking over the day's
adventures when they heard a
pitiful crying at the foot of the tree.
"James!" cried Harriet.
He was crouching under the bushes,
all scratched and bleeding, and one of
his wings dragged upon the ground.
"It was the Owl," he said, when
his sisters had helped him climb painfully
up the tree trunk to their home hole. "I just escaped.
She caught me, but I scratched her, and she let go for
a moment."

And just then Roger came scrambling into the nest
with his eyes round and black and full of fear. "She's
after me!" he cried. "The Owl!"

They all washed James's wounds till he fell asleep.

"Now we know how the little birds feel," said Thelma, grimly.

"What will James do?" Harriet whispered. "Will he ever fly again?"

"He'd better not," said a soft, large voice just outside their door. The Owl was sitting there.

The Tabbies looked at one another. They did not say a word till morning came.

At sunrise Thelma peered cautiously out. The Owl was gone. "Until this evening," said Thelma.

From then on they had to hunt in the daytime and hide in their nest all night; for the Owl thinks slowly, but the Owl thinks long.

James was ill for days and could not hunt at all. When he recovered, he was very thin and could not fly much, for his left wing soon grew stiff and lame. He never complained. He sat for hours by the creek, his wings folded, fishing. The fish did not complain either. They never do.

One night of early summer the Tabbies were all curled in their home hole, rather tired and discouraged. A raccoon family was quarreling loudly in the next tree. Thelma had found nothing to eat all day but a shrew, which gave her indigestion. A coyote had chased Roger away from the wood rat he had been about to catch that afternoon. James's fishing had been unsuccessful. The Owl kept flying past on silent wings, saying nothing.

Two young male raccoons in the next tree started a fight, cursing and shouting insults. The other raccoons all joined in, screeching and scratching and swearing.

"It sounds just like the old alley," James remarked.

"Do you remember the Shoes?" Harriet asked dreamily. She was looking quite plump, perhaps because she was so small. Her sister and brothers had become thin and rather scruffy.

"Yes," James said. "Some of them chased me once."

"Do you remember the Hands?"
Roger asked.

"Yes," Thelma said. "Some of
them picked me up once. When I was
just a kitten."

"What did they do—the Hands?"
Harriet asked.

"They squeezed me. It hurt. And
the hands person was shouting—'Wings!
Wings! It has wings!'—that's what it kept
shouting in its silly voice. And squeezing me."

"What did you do?"

"I bit it," Thelma said, with modest pride. "I bit it,
and it dropped me, and I ran back to Mother, under
the dumpster. I didn't know how to fly yet."

"I saw one today," said Harriet.

"What? A Hands? A Shoes?" said Thelma.

"A human bean?" said James.

"A human being?" Roger said.

"Yes," said Harriet. "It saw me, too."

"Did it chase you?"

"Did it kick you?"

"Did it throw things at you?"

"No. It just stood and watched me flying. And its
eyes got round, just like ours."

"Mother always said," Thelma remarked,
thoughtfully, "that if you found the right kind of
Hands, you'd never have to hunt again. But if you
found the wrong kind, it would be worse than dogs,
she said."

"I think this one is the right kind," said Harriet.

"What makes you think so?" Roger asked, sounding like their mother.

"Because it ran off and came back with a plate full of dinner," Harriet said. "And it put the dinner down on that big stump at the edge of the field, the field where we scared the cows that day, you know. And then it went off quite a way, and sat down, and just watched me. So I flew over and ate the dinner. It was an interesting dinner. Like what we used to get in the alley, but fresher. And," said Harriet, sounding like their mother, "I'm going back there tomorrow and see what's on that stump."

"You just be careful, Harriet Tabby!" said Thelma, sounding even more like their mother.

THE NEXT DAY, when Harriet went to the big stump at the edge of the cow pasture, flying low and cautiously, she found a tin pie-plate of meat scraps and kibbled catfood waiting for her. The girl from Overhill Farm was also waiting for her, sitting about twenty feet away from the stump, and holding very still. Susan Brown was her name, and she was eight years old. She watched Harriet fly out of the woods and hover like a fat hummingbird over the stump, then settle down, fold her wings neatly, and eat. Susan Brown held her breath. Her eyes grew round.

The next day, when Harriet and Roger flew cautiously out of the woods and hovered over the stump, Susan was sitting about fifteen feet away, and beside her sat her twelve-year-old brother Hank. He had not believed a word she said about flying cats. Now his eyes were perfectly round, and he was holding his breath.

Harriet and Roger settled down to eat.

"You didn't say there were two of them," Hank whispered to his sister.

Harriet and Roger sat on the stump licking their whiskers clean.

"You didn't say there were two of them," Roger whispered to his sister.

"I didn't know!" both the sisters whispered back. "There was only one, yesterday. But they look nice—don't they?"

The next day, Hank and Susan put out two pie-tins of cat dinner on the stump, then went ten steps away, sat down in the grass, and waited.

Harriet flew boldly from the woods and alighted on the stump. Roger followed her. Then—"Oh, look!" Susan whispered—came Thelma, flying very slowly, with a disapproving expression on her face. And finally—"Oh, look, *look!*" Susan whispered—James, flying low and lame, flapped over to the stump, landed on it, and began to eat. He ate, and ate, and ate. He

even growled once at Thelma, who moved to the other
pie-tin.

The two children watched the four winged cats.

Harriet, quite full, washed her face, and watched
the children.

Thelma finished a last tasty kibble, washed her
left front paw, and gazed at the children. Suddenly
she flew up from the stump and straight at them. They
ducked as she went over. She flew right round both
their heads and then back to the stump.

"Testing," she said to Harriet, James, and Roger.

"If she does it again, don't catch her," Hank said to Susan. "It'd scare her off."

"You think I'm *stupid?*" Susan hissed.

They sat still. The cats sat still. Cows ate grass nearby. The sun shone.

"Kitty," Susan said in a soft, high voice. "Kitty kit-kit-kit-kit-kit-cat, kitty-cat, kittywings, kittywings, catwings!"

Harriet jumped off the stump into the air, performed a cartwheel, and flew loop-the-loop over to Susan. She landed on Susan's shoulder and sat there, holding on tight and purring in Susan's ear.

"I will never never never ever catch you, or cage you, or do anything to you you don't want me to do," Susan said to Harriet. "I promise. Hank, you promise too."

"Purr," said Harriet.

"I promise. And we'll never ever tell anybody else," Hank said, rather fiercely. "Ever! Because—you know how people are. If people saw them—"

"I promise," Susan said. She and Hank shook hands, promising.

Roger flew gracefully over and landed on Hank's shoulder.

"Purr," said Roger.

"They could live in the old barn," Susan said. "Nobody ever goes there but us. There's that dovecote up in the loft, with all those holes in the wall where the doves flew in and out."

"We can take hay up there and make them a place to sleep," Hank said.

"Purr," said Roger.

Very softly and gently Hank raised his hand and stroked Roger right between the wings.

"Oooh," said James, watching. He jumped down off the stump and came trotting over to the children. He sat down near Susan's shoes. Very softly and gently Susan reached down and scratched James under the chin and behind the ears.

"Purr," James said, and drooled a little on Susan's shoe.

"Oh, well!" said Thelma, having cleaned up the last of the cold roast beef. She arose in the air, flew over with great dignity, sat right down in Hank's lap, folded her wings, and said, "Purr, purr, purr . . ."

"Oh, Hank," Susan whispered, "their wings are furry."

"Oh, James," Harriet whispered, "their hands are kind."

Pulling the Theme Together

IMAGINATION

1. Dig your claws in. Which of these things captured your interest? Why?
  flying tabbies
  leaving home
  town and country
  dangers
  unknown hardships

2. In this book you've read about several different ways people can use their imaginations. Which character or person in these selections strikes you as being most imaginative? Why? Justify your response.

3. The characters, authors, and illustrators in this book really used their imaginations! What would you like to do that's imaginative? Draw a picture? Invent a machine? Write a fantasy? Or something completely different? Explain your choice.

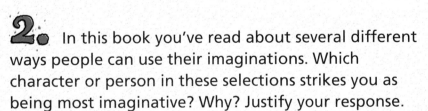

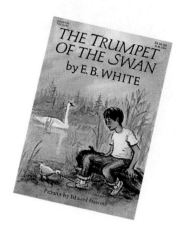

**Jason and the Escape from
Bat Planet**
*by Gery Greer and
Bob Ruddick*
HarperCollins, 1993
Jason Harkness and the
Intergalactic Troubleshooting
Team are off on a rescue
mission to face the Demon Bats
of Bluggax. Cooper Vor, the
team's leader, has a plan . . .
sort of.

**Your Mother Was
a Neanderthal**
by Jon Scieszka
Viking, 1993
The Time Warp Trio is back,
and this time they're checking
out prehistoric times. The plan
is to impress the people of the
Stone Age, but with these guys,
nothing ever goes as planned.

The Trumpet of the Swan
by E. B. White
Harper, 1970
Life is really a challenge for a
trumpeter swan who is born
without a voice. Has he got
what it takes to wind up a
winner?

Under the Sunday Tree
by Eloise Greenfield
Harper, 1988
Let the rich poetry and beautiful
pictures take you to a warm,
sunny island surrounded by the
brightest, bluest water you've
ever seen.

★

Mariah Delany's Author-of-the-Month Club
by Sheila Greenwald
Little, Brown, 1990
Mariah invites famous authors to tell "the stories behind their stories." With such a terrific idea, how could things backfire?

Flossie and the Fox
by Patricia McKissack
Dial, 1986
A conniving Fox wants the eggs Flossie carries in her basket, but Flossie isn't easily foxed. A great read-aloud tale—and be sure to show the pictures.

★

The Tale of the Mandarin Ducks
by Katherine Paterson
Dutton, 1990
"Floating world" art and a strange story of kindness rewarded make this a book to share with friends and to remember always.

Black and White
by David Macaulay
Houghton Mifflin, 1990
In this upside-down, inside-out adventure book, you won't know whether you're reading one story or four until it all comes together in the end. Or does it?

★

Literary Terms

ESSAY

An **essay** is a composition that is written to explain something to you or convince you that it is true. The Dillons' essay, "Through the Eyes of the Illustrators," explains how they get their ideas and how they turn their ideas into art. Essays can also be written to discuss a topic or a variety of topics.

FANTASY

A **fantasy** is a story that could not really happen. All fantasies have realistic elements: sometimes the characters, or the setting, or even parts of the plot seem real. In "Laughing Gas,"

the characters—Jane and Michael, Mr. Wigg and Mary Poppins—seem like ordinary people. That is, they seem normal except, of course, that they can float up to the ceiling and sit there while they have tea. One way an author produces fantasy is to give the characters unusual or superhuman powers. That is what Pamela Travers did with the *Mary Poppins* stories. A fantasy can also be a story told in folk tale style, or a tale of pure imagination with talking animals and objects that come alive.

PLOT

When we speak of **plot,** we're really talking about two things: the order of how things happen and the struggles or conflicts of characters in the story. In *Catwings,* the plot develops as we see the kittens struggling against nature. At first they must get away from an unsafe, crowded home where dogs and people threaten their lives. Later, in the country, they must hunt for their food and escape an unfriendly owl. The cats' problem is resolved when they are discovered by two children whom they feel are trustworthy.

SETTING

The **setting** of a story is, quite simply, where and when it takes place. A setting is described in words and illustrations. At the beginning of *Catwings,* the setting is the city. The family lives near a garbage dumpster. When the kittens fly away to a better home, they are surprised to land on dirt, not on pavement. That is a clue that the setting has changed to the country. Notice how different the description is. There are trees and a creek and a cow pasture in the country setting. Another important element of setting is time: when the story takes place. In "Laughing Gas," the characters' clothing and natural gas light fixtures clue us that this story is set many years ago.

THEME

The **theme** is the most important idea running through an entire piece of writing. The theme holds the piece together so that all of its parts fit around that idea. Julio, in "Julio, That's Who!" manages to convince the principal that the students should be allowed to play soccer at recess. During the campaign for president, he argues that the students, not the teacher, should decide how to spend the money they earn as a class. Using your imagination to get others to agree with you is the main idea, or theme, that runs through the story.

Glossary

How to Use the Pronunciation Key

After each entry word in this glossary, there is a special spelling, called the **pronunciation.** It shows how to say the word. The word is broken into syllables and then spelled with letters and signs. You can look up these letters and signs in the **pronunciation key** to see what sounds they stand for.

This dark mark (ʹ) is called the **primary accent.** It follows the syllable you say with the most force. This lighter mark (ʹ) is the **secondary accent.** Say the syllable it follows with medium force. Syllables without marks are said with least force.

Vocabulary from your selections

a	hat	i	it	oi	oil	ch	child	ə stands for:
ā	age	ī	ice	ou	out	ng	long	a in about
ä	far	o	hot	u	cup	sh	she	e in taken
e	let	ō	open	ú	put	th	thin	i in pencil
ē	equal	ô	order	ü	rule	ᴛʜ	then	o in lemon
ėr	term					zh	measure	u in circus

bard (bärd), **1** poet and singer of long ago: *The bard sang his own poems to the music of his harp.* **2** any poet. *n.* [*Bard* comes from Irish and Scottish Gaelic *bard.*]

bar gain (bär′gən), **1** agreement to trade or exchange; deal: *You can't back out on our bargain.* **2** something offered for sale cheap or bought cheap: *This hat is a bargain.* **3** try to get good terms; try to make a good deal: *I bargained with the owner and bought the book for $5 instead of $8.* 1,2 *n.,* 3 *v.* —**bar′gain er,** *n.*

bob (bob), **1** move up and down, or to and fro, with short, quick motions: *The pigeon bobbed its head as it picked up crumbs.* **2** a short, quick motion up and down, or to and fro. 1 *v.,* **bobbed, bob bing;** 2 *n.*
bob up, appear suddenly or unexpectedly.

brain storm (brān′stôrm′), INFORMAL. a sudden idea or inspiration. *n.*

cam paign (kam pān′), **1** series of related military operations in a war which are aimed at some special purpose: *The general planned a campaign to capture the enemy's most important city.* **2** series of connected activities to do or get something: *Our town had a campaign to raise money for a new hospital.* **3** take part or serve in a campaign: *She campaigned for mayor by giving speeches.* 1,2 *n.,* 3 *v.* —**cam paign′er,** *n.*

can di date (kan′də dāt), person who seeks, or is proposed for, some office or honor: *There are three candidates for president of the club. n.*

chant (chant), **1** a short, simple song in which several syllables or words are sung in one tone. Chants are sometimes used in religious services. **2** keep talking about; say over and over again: *The football fans chanted, "Go, team, go!"* 1 *n.,* 2 *v.*
—**chant′er,** *n.* —**chant′ing ly,** *adv.*

clan (klan), **1** group of related families that claim to be descended from a common ancestor. **2** group of people closely joined together by some common interest: *The whole clan of jazz fans was at the concert. n.*
—**clan′like′,** *adj.*

com pe ti tion (kom′pə tish′ən), **1** a trying hard to win or gain something wanted by others; rivalry: *competition among stores for customers.* **2** contest: *She won first place in the swimming competition. n.*

con vince (kən vins′), make (a person) feel sure; cause to believe; persuade by argument or proof: *The mistakes she made convinced me she had not studied her lesson. v.,* **con vinced, con vinc ing.** —**con vinc′er,** *n.*
—**con vin′ci ble,** *adj.*

drape (drāp), **1** cover or hang with cloth falling loosely in folds, especially as a decoration: *The buildings were draped with red, white, and blue bunting.* **2** arrange (clothes, hangings, etc.) to hang loosely in folds: *The actor draped the cape over his shoulders. v.,* **draped, drap ing.**

A Roman toga was worn **draped** over the shoulder.

ef fect (ə fekt′), **1** whatever is produced by a cause; something made to happen by a person or thing; result: *The effect of their research was a new kind of plastic.* **2** make happen; bring about: *Florence Nightingale effected many changes in nursing.* **3** power to produce results; force; influence: *The medicine had an immediate effect.* **4** impression produced on the mind or senses: *The room was painted yellow for a light, sunny effect.* **5** something which produces such an impression: *The movie used many special effects to make its scenes appear real.* 1,3-5 *n.,* 2 *v.* —**ef fect′er,** *n.*
for effect, for show; in order to impress or influence others: *He said that only for effect; he really didn't mean it.*
in effect, 1 almost the same as; practically; virtually: *By not speaking out against this plan you are saying, in effect, that you approve it.* **2** in force or operation; active: *That law has been in effect for two years.*

ex per i ment (ek sper′ə ment), try in order to find out; make trials or tests: *The painter is experimenting with different paints to get the color she wants. v.* —**ex per′i ment′er,** *n.*

ex tinc tion (ek stingk′shən), **1** an extinguishing: *The sudden extinction of the lights left the room in darkness.* **2** bringing to an end; wiping out; destruction: *Physicians are working toward the extinction of many serious diseases. n.*

gadg et (gaj′it), a small mechanical device or contrivance; any ingenious device: *Can openers and cookie cutters are kitchen gadgets. n.*

gadgets

glide (glīd), **1** move along smoothly, evenly, and easily: *Birds, ships, dancers, and skaters glide.* **2** a smooth, even, easy movement. 1 *v.,* **glid ed, glid ing;** 2 *n.*

hard ship (härd′ship), something hard to bear; hard condition of living: *Hunger, cold, and sickness were among the hardships of pioneer life. n.*

i dle (ī′dl), **1** doing nothing; not busy; not working: *the idle hours of a holiday, idle hands.* **2** fond of doing nothing; not willing to work; lazy: *an idle student.* **3** useless; worthless: *to waste time in idle pleasures.* **4** without any good reason: *idle rumors.* **5** be idle; do nothing: *Are you going to spend your whole vacation just idling?* 1-4 *adj.,* **i dler, i dlest;** 5 *v.,* **i dled, i dling.** —**i′dle ness,** *n.*

il lus tra tion (il′ə strā′shən), **1** picture, diagram, map, etc., used to explain or decorate something. **2** story, example, comparison, etc., used to make clear or explain something: *An apple cut into four equal pieces is a good illustration of what ¼ means.* **3** act or process of illustrating: *Her illustration of how to build a bookcase taught us a lot. n.*

il lus tra tor (il′ə strā′tər), artist who makes pictures to be used as illustrations. *n.*

i mag i na tion (i maj′ə nā′shən), **1** power of forming pictures or images in the mind of things not present to the senses. A poet, artist, or inventor must have imagination to create new things or ideas or to combine old ones in new forms. **2** thing imagined; fancy. *n.*

in no va tion (in′ə vā′shən), making changes; bringing in new things or new ways of doing things: *Many people are opposed to innovation. n.*

in vent (in vent′), **1** make up for the first time; think out (something new): *Alexander Graham Bell invented the telephone.* **2** make up; think up: *Since they had no good reason for being late, they invented an excuse. v.*

in ven tion (in ven′shən), **1** a making something new: *the invention of gunpowder.* **2** thing invented: *Television is a modern invention.* **3** power of inventing: *An author must have invention to think up new ideas for stories.* **4** a made-up story; false statement: *That rumor is merely invention. n.*

Alexander Graham Bell and his **invention** the telephone.

lar i at (lar′ē ət), a long rope with a noose at the end, used for catching horses and cattle; lasso. *n.* [*Lariat* comes from Spanish *la reata,* meaning "the rope."]

lariat

a hat	i it	oi oil	ch child	ə stands for:
ā age	ī ice	ou out	ng long	a in about
ä far	o hot	u cup	sh she	e in taken
e let	ō open	ủ put	th thin	i in pencil
ē equal	ô order	ü rule	ᴛʜ then	o in lemon
ėr term			zh measure	u in circus

light (līt), **1** come down to the ground; alight: *light from a horse.* **2** come down from flight: *A bird lighted on the branch.* **3** come by chance: *Her eye lighted upon a coin in the road. v.,* **light ed** or **lit, light ing.**

man age (man′ij), **1** to guide or handle with skill or authority; control; direct: *manage a business, manage an election campaign, manage a horse.* **2** succeed in accomplishing; contrive; arrange: *I shall manage to keep warm. v.,* **man aged, man ag ing.**

man ag er (man′ə jər), person who manages, especially one who manages a business: *She is the manager of the department store. n.*

mirth (mėrth), merry fun; being joyous or gay; laughter. *n.*

mood (müd), state of mind or feeling: *I am in the mood to play now; I don't want to study. n.*

nar ra tor (nar′ā tər *or* na rā′tər), person who tells a story. *n.*

nom i na tion (nom′ə nā′shən), **1** a naming as a candidate for office: *The nominations for president of the club were written on the blackboard.* **2** selection for office or duty; appointment to office or duty. *n.*

ob serve (əb zėrv′), **1** see and note; notice: *I observed nothing strange in her behavior.* **2** examine for some special purpose; study: *An astronomer observes the stars.* **3** to remark; comment: *"Bad weather ahead,"* she *observed. v.,* **ob served, ob serv ing.**

ob serv er (əb zėr′vər), person who observes. *n.*

ob serv ing (əb zėr′ving), observant; quick to notice. *adj.* —**ob serv′ing ly,** *adv.*

old-fash ioned (ōld′fash′ənd), **1** out of date in style, construction, etc.; of or typical of an old style or time: *an old-fashioned dress.* **2** keeping to old ways, ideas, etc.: *They are very old-fashioned in their ideas. adj.*

par tic i pant (pär tis′ə pənt), person who shares or participates. *n.*

par tic i pate (pär tis′ə pāt), have a share; take part: *The teacher participated in the children's games. v.,* **par tic i pat ed, par tic i pat ing.** [*Participate* can be traced back to Latin *partem,* meaning "a part, share," and *capere,* meaning "to take."] —**par tic′i pat′ing ly,** *adv.*

pat ent (pat′nt), a government document which gives a person or company sole rights to make, use, or sell a new invention for a certain number of years. *n.,* —**pat′ent a ble,** *adj.*

re flect (ri flekt′), **1** turn back or throw back (light, heat, sound, etc.): *The sidewalks reflect heat on a hot day.* **2** give back a likeness or image of: *The sky was reflected in the still pond.* **3** reproduce or show like a mirror: *The newspaper reflected the owner's opinions.* **4** think carefully: *Take time to reflect before making a decision.* **5** cast blame, reproach, or discredit: *The children's spoiled behavior reflected on their parents.* **6** serve to cast or bring: *A kind act reflects credit on the person who does it. v.* —**re flect′ing ly,** *adv.*

rep re sent (rep′ri zent′), **1** stand for; be a sign or symbol of: *The 50 stars in our flag represent the 50 states.* **2** act in place of; speak and act for: *We chose a committee to represent us.* **3** act the part of: *Each child will represent an animal at the party. v.* —**rep′re sent′a ble,** *adj.*

re spond (ri spond′), **1** answer; reply: *He responded to the question.* **2** act in answer; react: *A dog responds to kind treatment by loving its owner. v.*

re store (ri stôr′), **1** bring back; establish again: *The police restored order.* **2** bring back to a former condition or to a normal condition:

The old house has been restored. **3** give back; put back: *The boy restored the money he had found to its owner. v.,* **re stored, re stor ing.** —**re stor′a ble,** *adj.*

root (rüt *or* rut), **1** the part of a plant that grows downward, usually into the ground, to hold the plant in place, absorb water and mineral foods from the soil, and often to store food material. **2** any underground part of a plant. **3** something like a root in shape, position, use, etc.: *the root of a tooth, the roots of the hair.* **4** a part from which other things grow and develop; cause; source: *"The love of money is the root of all evil."* **5** send out roots and begin to grow; become fixed in the ground: *Some plants root more quickly than others.* **6** fix firmly: *He was rooted to the spot by surprise.* **7** become firmly fixed. **8** pull, tear, or dig (up, out, etc.) by the roots; get completely rid of. **9** the essential part; base. *n.*

The **roots** of a plant

run (run), **1** go by moving the legs quickly; go faster than walking: *A horse can run faster than a person.* **2** go in a hurry; hasten: *Run for help.* **3** make a quick trip: *Let's run over to the lake for the weekend.* **4** escape; flee: *Run for your life.* **5** cause to run; cause to move: *run a horse up and down a track.* **6** do by running: *run a race, run errands.* **7** take part in a race or contest. **8** be a candidate for election: *run for class president. v.*

self ish (sel′fish), **1** caring too much for oneself; caring too little for others.

Selfish people put their own interests first. **2** showing care solely or chiefly for oneself: *selfish motives. adj.* —**self′ish ly,** *adv.* —**self′ish ness,** *n.*

ser i ous (sir′ē əs), **1** showing deep thought or purpose; thoughtful; grave: *a serious manner, a serious face.* **2** in earnest; not fooling; sincere: *Are you joking or are you serious?* **3** needing thought; important: *Choice of one's lifework is a serious matter.* **4** important because it may do much harm; dangerous: *The patient was in serious condition. adj.* —**ser′i ous ly,** *adv.* —**ser′i ous ness,** *n.*

step daugh ter (step′dô′tər), daughter of one's husband or wife by a former marriage. *n.*

style (stīl), **1** fashion: *Several popular teenagers set the style in dress at the school. My clothes are out of style.* **2** manner; method; way: *the Gothic style of architecture. She learned several styles of swimming.* **3** way of writing or speaking: *Books for children should have a clear, easy style.* **4** good style: *She dresses in style.* **5** excellence of form or expression in literature, speech, art, etc.: *a model of style, a master of literary style.* **6** make in or conform to a given or accepted style; stylize: *Her poem is styled with care.* **7** to design according to a style or fashion: *His suits are styled by a famous designer.* **8** to name; call: *She styles herself a poet.* 1-5 *n.,* 6-8 *v.,* **styled, styl ing.** —**style′less,** *adj.* —**style′like′,** *adj.* —**styl′er,** *n.*

tab by (tab′ē), **1** a gray or tawny cat with dark stripes. **2** a female cat. *n., pl.* **tab bies.**

tabby

trans fer (tran sfėr′ or tran′sfėr′ for 1,2,5; tran′sfėr′ for 3,4,6,7), **1** change or move from one person or place to another; hand over: *The clerk was transferred to another department. Please have my trunks transferred to the Union Station.* **2** convey (a drawing, design, pattern) from one surface to another: *You transfer the embroidery design from the paper to cloth by pressing it with a warm iron.* **3** a transferring or a being transferred. **4** thing transferred; a drawing, pattern, etc., printed from one surface onto another. **5** change from one bus, train, etc., to another. **6** ticket allowing a passenger to change from one bus, train, etc., to another. **7** point or place for transferring. 1,2,5 *v.,* **trans ferred, trans fer ring;** 3,4,6,7 *n.*

un dig′ni fied *see* dignified.

whirl wind (hwėrl′wind′), current of air whirling violently round and round; whirling windstorm. *n.*

wor ry (wėr′ē), **1** feel anxious; be uneasy: *Don't worry about little things. They will worry if we are late.* **2** make anxious; trouble: *The problem worried me.* **3** anxiety; uneasiness; trouble; care: *Worry kept me awake.* **4** cause of trouble or care: *Parents of a sick child have many worries.* **5** annoy; bother; vex: *Don't worry me right now with so many questions.* **6** seize and shake with the teeth; bite at; snap at: *The cat worried the mouse.* 1,2,5,6 *v.,* **wor ried, wor ry ing;** 3,4 *n., pl.* **wor ries.** —**wor′ri less,** *adj.* —**wor′ry ing ly,** *adv.*

Acknowledgments

Text

Page 6: From *Class President* by Johanna Hurwitz. Text copyright © 1990 by Johanna Hurwitz. Reprinted by permission of William Morrow and Company, Inc.

Page 26: "What a Wild Idea" by Louis Sabin, illustrated by Christine Mortensen from *Boys' Life*, September 1990. Reprinted by permission.

Page 32: "I'm Tipingee, She's Tipingee, We're Tipingee, Too" is from *Reader's Theatre: Plays and Poems to Read Aloud*. Copyright © 1987 by Caroline Feller Bauer. Reprinted by permission of the H.W. Wilson Company, New York and Alfred A. Knopf, Inc. (Dr. Bauer's play is adapted from the short story of the same name in *The Magic Orange Tree and Other Haitian Folktales*. Copyright © 1978 by Diane Wolkstein.)

Page 42: "The Voice of Africa in American Music," by Jim Haskins. Copyright © 1991 by Jim Haskins.

Page 50: "Through the Eyes of the Illustrators," by Leo and Diane Dillon. Copyright © 1991 by Leo and Diane Dillon.

Page 52: Illustration from *The Tale of the Mandarin Ducks* by Katherine Paterson, pictures by Leo and Diane Dillon. Pictures © 1990 by Leo and Diane Dillon. Used by permission of Lodestar Books, an affiliate of Dutton Children's Books, a division of Penguin Books USA Inc.

Page 53: Illustration by Leo & Diane Dillon to accompany *Two Pair of Shoes* retold by P. L. Travers. Reproduced by permission of Leo & Diane Dillon.

Page 54: Illustration from *Why Mosquitoes Buzz in People's Ears* by Verna Aardema, pictures by Leo and Diane Dillon. Pictures copyright © 1975 by Leo and Diane Dillon. Used by permission of Dial Books for Young Readers, a division of Penguin Books USA Inc.

Page 57: Illustration from *The Porcelain Cat* by Michael Patrick Hearn with illustrations by Leo and Diane Dillon. Illustrations copyright © 1985 by Leo and Diane Dillon. By permission of Little, Brown and Company.

Page 60: *The Third Gift* by Jan Carew, with illustrations by Leo and Diane Dillon. Text copyright © 1974 by Jan Carew. Illustrations copyright © 1974 by Leo and Diane Dillon. By permission of Little, Brown and Company.

Page 74: From *Whirlwind Is a Ghost Dancing* by Natalia Belting, illustrated by Leo and Diane Dillon. Text copyright © 1974 by Natalia Belting. Illustrations copyright © 1974 by Leo and Diane Dillon. Used by permission of Dutton Children's Books, a division of Penguin Books USA Inc.

Page 78: From *Ashanti to Zulu: African Traditions* by Margaret Musgrove, pictures by Leo and Diane Dillon. Text copyright © 1976 by Margaret Musgrove. Pictures copyright © 1976 by Leo and Diane Dillon. Used by permission of Dial Books for Young Readers, a division of Penguin Books USA Inc.

Page 84: Text and illustrations from "Laughing Gas" in *Mary Poppins*, copyright © 1934 and renewed 1962 by P. L. Travers, reprinted by permission of Harcourt Brace & Company.

Page 100: "How Did Mary Poppins Find Me?" by P. L. Travers from *Cricket Magazine*, December 1973. Copyright © 1973 by P. L. Travers. Reprinted by permission of Harold Ober Associates.

Illustrations from *Mary Poppins*, copyright © 1934 and renewed 1962 by P. L. Travers, reprinted by permission of Harcourt Brace Jovanovich, Inc.

Page 103 (top): Illustration by Mary Shepard in *Mary Poppins Comes Back*, copyright © 1935 and renewed 1962 by P. L. Travers, reproduced by permission of Harcourt Brace & Company.

Page 104: *Catwings* by Ursula K. Le Guin. Text copyright © 1988 by Ursula K. Le Guin. Illustrations copyright © 1988 by S. D. Schindler. All rights reserved. Reprinted by permission of Orchard Books, New York.

Artists

Illustrations owned and copyrighted by the illustrator.
Johnston Clark, Cover, pages 1–3
Steve Snodgrass, 6–24
Fritz Millevoix, 32–41
Leo and Diane Dillon, 50–83
Mary Shepard, 84, 94, 96, 99, 102, 103
Greg Thompson (lettering), 84–124
S. D. Schindler, 104–124

Photographs

Photographs not listed were shot by ScottForesman.
Page 43: Jason Laure
Page 44: Jack Vartoogian
Page 46 (ALL): The Granger Collection
Page 47: Jazzmen Photo, Ramsey Archives
Page 48: Dennis Brack/Black Star
Page 49 (ALL): The Granger Collection
Page 51: Courtesy Leo and Diane Dillon
Page 100: Privately taken
Page 131: Courtesy Alinari
Page 133т: Courtesy Brown Brothers
Page 133в: *Cowboy Roping Steer*—Charles Russell—Woolaroc Museum, Bartlesville, Oklahoma

Glossary

The contents of the Glossary entries in this book have been adapted from *Intermediate Dictionary*, Copyright © 1988 Scott, Foresman and Company; and *Advanced Dictionary*, Copyright © 1988 Scott, Foresman and Company.